KNOWING THE KNOWER

KNOWING THE KNOWER

A JÑĀNA YOGA MANUAL

SWAMI TYAGANANDA

PREFACE

After writing *Walking the Walk,* it was inevitable that I'd start thinking about a follow-up, and *Knowing the Knower* is the result. Two more manuals are likely, covering the remaining two yogas of Swami Vivekananda, rounding off the series on Yoga Manuals. There is no special reason for the order in which I am attempting to write the commentaries on these four yogas. Each yoga is in itself a complete path to spiritual freedom but, in Vivekananda's interpretation of Vedanta, no yoga is completely independent of the other yogas.

Every one of Vivekananda's four yogas is a set of spiritual disciplines that is woven around a specific function of the mind. The mind has three primary functions: the conative (manifests as will-power), the affective (manifests as the power of emotions), and the cognitive (manifests as the power of reason).

Karma yoga represents practices that purify the will-power by engaging with the *external* world through work.

Raja yoga represents practices which also purify the will-power but by engaging with the *internal* world through meditation. Bhakti yoga represents practices that purify the power of emotions through love of God. Jñāna yoga, the subject of our present study, represents practices that purify the power of reason through discernment.

While it is only natural that one or more of these powers may dominate over others in a person's mental makeup, it is also true that none of these powers is totally absent in any mind. Every yoga highlights a specific function of the mind, but other functions do play subsidiary roles in each of the yogas—which is why no yoga can be said to be completely independent of the other yogas. Nor is any of the yogas superior to any other yoga, although such claims are made from time to time. Every yoga is inherently capable of revealing the highest truth to the practitioner who is fit for its practice.

There is also the popular notion that jñāna yoga is more "difficult" as opposed to bhakti yoga which is "easy." The truth is that no yoga is difficult or easy in itself. As in most things in life, the level of interest and aptitude are what make the difference. A person who has interest in a specific yoga and sufficient aptitude to practice it will find that yoga "easy." If not, the same yoga will appear to be "difficult."

In the nine volumes of Swami Vivekananda's *Complete Works*, a set of ten lectures form a section called "Jnana Yoga," which is also available as a stand-alone book. It

was first published in 1897 in Chennai as a collection of
classes given in New York and London: the book was
titled *Lectures on Gnana Yoga*. In 1902 another version was
published in Kolkata with a somewhat different
collection of lectures. The Vedanta Society in New York
published yet another version in two parts (1902 and
1907). The text of *Jnana Yoga* as it is available today was
put together in 1907 for the first edition of the second
volume of the *Complete Works*. All of the versions were
distinct but their contents shared much in common.[1]

It would be a mistake, though, to limit Swami
Vivekananda's exposition of jñāna yoga to only what is
included in the books under that title. His invaluable
insights on the subject are spread throughout his *Complete
Works* and all of those must be taken into account while
studying the subject. Consider, for instance, his
"Discourses on Jnana Yoga" (CW 8. 3–35) and
"Inspired Talks" (CW 7. 3–104), both of which were
given in New York in the spring and summer of 1895,
and are not a part of the book *Jnana Yoga*.[2]

The structure of the present book is simple. The first
chapter deals with knowledge, and more specifically with
the knowledge of who we really are. The second chapter
discusses ignorance and its powers—and how ignorance
of our true identity affects our lives. Every one of
Swami Vivekananda's four yogas has a "key" to unlock
its secrets. Jñāna yoga's key is discernment—and that is
what the third chapter focuses on. It examines the kinds
of questions we ask about God, about the world and
about ourselves—and how discernment helps us come

to grips with those questions and rediscover who we really are.

All of our problems can be traced back to a kind of forgetfulness of our self-identity. If ignorance is the root problem, knowledge is the obvious solution. It would seem, therefore, that there is nothing really we need to do about it other than just to know the truth. Right, but what if our knowledge remains theoretical and merely stimulates the intellect? What if it doesn't bring about any real transformation in our lives? Then we must to do something about it. What we need to do is to know the truth so deeply, entering into it fully as it were, that it is no longer limited to *having* the knowledge but *being* it. That needs practice, which is the focus of chapter four.

While the first three chapters deal with the basic theoretical structure of jñāna yoga, the fourth chapter is really the heart of this manual. All the readings on Vedanta and the discussions that result from them are futile if they are not backed by practice. Not for nothing did Vivekananda say that "an ounce of practice is worth a thousand pounds of theory."[3] My hope is that readers will begin at least some form of practice after reading this book. After all, what we gain from practice is ours for ever. What we gain from reading is ours only as long as we remember it.

The last chapter is about the goal of jñāna yoga. What does the practice of jñāna yoga entail? How are we challenged when we begin the practice? How does our life change as the practice matures? Does attaining the

knowledge of the self do any good to the world?—such
are the questions addressed in the concluding chapter.

The inspiration behind this manual is Swami
Vivekananda's teachings found in his *Complete Works*
—specifically, in the set of lectures in the book titled
Jnana Yoga. This manual is not meant to replace the
book, but it can be read as a commentary on
Vivekananda's insights on the subject. In the course of
time, other commentaries will no doubt be written,
providing different perspectives and probing the yoga of
knowledge to deeper depths. The endnotes to this book
primarily reference specific passages from the *Complete
Works* (abbreviated as CW) on which the commentary is
based. Additional information and thoughts are also
moved to the endnotes to keep the book's central
narrative uninterrupted and concise.

I have tried to keep the use of Sanskrit terms to a
minimum, preferring to use English equivalents for easy
reading. The only exception to this has been the use of
"Ātman" instead of "self." This has helped avoid the
sometimes confusing subtlety involved in making the
distinction between the lower-cased self and the
capitalized Self. Moreover, the concept of the Ātman is
unique to Vedanta. One may go so far as to claim that it
is Vedanta's contribution to the rich and diverse field of
religion. So it seemed appropriate to privilege the
Sanskrit term over its English translation "self," which in
any case has several connotations depending on the
context.[4]

Swami Vivekananda's exposition of Vedanta is sometimes characterized as Neo-Vedanta. The term has always puzzled me and raised the question: "neo" with respect to what? There has never been a Vedanta cast in stone compared to which a later version can be termed Neo-Vedanta. Vedanta is a living entity: it is always growing, evolving, and responding to the changing horizons of the material world. Vedanta renews itself constantly even as its core remains unchanged. At no point in history—and at no place on this planet—has Vedanta remained frozen. Employing the term Neo-Vedanta doesn't add anything new to our understanding. It only serves to obfuscate a clear and coherent study of both Vedanta and Vivekananda.

When I lived in Chennai in the 1980s, I had the chance to study all over again the basic texts of Vedanta with a teacher who was untouched by modern systems of education. Trained from his childhood in a traditional, orthodox Vedic school, Sri V. Kalyanasundara Sastrigal (1911–98) was a magnificent Vedanta teacher whose scholarship was matched only by his heartfelt humility. Studying under his guidance and comparing what I learned from him with my understanding of Vivekananda, I realized in a powerful way that Vivekananda's teachings remained stubbornly true to Vedanta's roots while being amazingly universal in their reach and sensitive to contemporary concerns. It is to Sri Sastrigal that this little book is dedicated with gratitude.

KNOWLEDGE

*A*n earnest student named Śaunaka went to Sage Aṅgirasa and asked him, "Tell me, Master, what is that knowing which everything becomes known?"[1] This simple question from the Vedas provides a good starting point for the study of jñāna yoga, the spiritual discipline woven around the cognitive function of the mind.

It is easy to imagine Śaunaka's quandary. Hungry for knowledge, Śaunaka had realized that there were just too many things to be known but not enough time and energy to know them all. Wouldn't it be convenient if all we needed to know was just one thing, knowing which everything would become known? After all, it is possible to have a master key that opens all the doors in a house. Or a master password that unlocks all of my passwords. So Śaunaka's question is not unreasonable: Is there a master knowledge that will remove all of my ignorance in one stroke?

Not all may express their need in precisely the way
Śaunaka did. Whichever way it is expressed, we human
beings seem forever hungry for knowledge. Our seeking
after knowledge begins soon after birth. We can see it in
the eyes of a baby as she scans the world and people
around her. We can see it in the way a child turns the
pages of a book or, more likely today, swipes the pictures
on a smartphone or other mobile devices. We can see it
when students pore over library books, reporters cover
events for the media, chefs experiment with new recipes,
people browse through newspapers in coffee shops, and
the elderly swap stories in retirement homes. We can see
it when people are at work or on vacation, when they
are at their desk or on a hike, and when they are
conversing with friends or ruminating in solitude.

No matter where we are and no matter what we are
doing, we are always trying to *know* something. The only
difference, perhaps, is that while some people do it
consciously, most others do it unconsciously. In some the
hunger to know is intense and in others it is muted. But
the quest for knowledge seems inbuilt in living beings.

We wouldn't feel the need to know something if we
already knew it. Our quest for knowledge is an
admission of our lack of knowledge. Our desire to know
springs from our ignorance—more accurately, from the
knowledge of our ignorance. When we know something,
our ignorance regarding it is dispelled, just as when we
turn on the lights in a room, the darkness in that room is
dispelled.

KINDS OF KNOWLEDGE

When we begin to think deeply about knowledge, we quickly realize that the answers we get depend on the kind of questions we ask. The first obvious question is: *what is knowledge?* While we understand the meaning of "knowledge," it is not easy to explain what knowledge really is. It's one thing to know the meaning, it's quite another to define the term.

It might be easier to say what knowledge *does* than what knowledge *is*. As far as doing goes, knowledge removes ignorance and leads to freedom. Ignorance has the power to constrict our ability to think deeply or to do certain things. Knowledge removes the barrier and frees us from those limitations. Both "ignorance" and "freedom" need to be examined carefully in order to fully understand what knowledge is and what it does— and this is something we'll explore later in this book.

Another possible question is: *how does knowledge arise?* The answer is simple enough: it arises from our contact with the world. The world impinges on the mind as sensations of sight, sound, taste, smell and touch. To grasp each of these five sensations, we have five receptors, called senses (*indriya*): eyes, ears, tongue, nose and skin.[2] Because these senses are the first link in a process that leads to knowledge, they are called senses of knowledge (*jñana+indriya=jñānedriya*). When the sensations are fed to the mind, they form impressions (*saṁskāras*).

What the mind does is best described as pigeonholing. It compares a new impression with its store of past impressions and, when it finds a match, it files the new impression in the right box. For instance, when the eyes detect something, the sensation is carried to the mind, where it forms an impression and the filing process begins. When the mind finds, let's say, that the impression matches those in the box labeled "animal," it files the impression there, producing the knowledge: "This is an animal." The mind may further detect that it also matches a sub-category called "dog," producing the knowledge, "This animal is dog" or simply, "This is a dog."[3] The mind can also rearrange its stock of impressions, discover patterns and gain new insights.[4]

How deep a knowledge I have will depend on the number of impressions in my mind and how accurately those impressions have been filed. A mind with a rich store of organized impressions will tend to have greater knowledge than less endowed minds. Whatever the quality of the mind, it is always from "out there" that the sensations enter into it, form impressions, are placed in pigeonholes, and produce knowledge. When an impression is placed in a wrong pigeonhole, it leads to false knowledge, but knowledge nonetheless. This kind of "knowledge" is often more damaging than plain ignorance.

Most people spend their entire lives gathering knowledge of external objects.[5] A few, though, are not satisfied with what's out there. It doesn't quite quench their thirst for knowledge. So they turn their gaze inward in order to find what is "in here." Questions about what's out there never end and the task is never quite fulfilling. Many have found it more exciting to ask questions about one's own self: Who is this person asking questions about the world? Who is this person seeking knowledge? Such questions concern not the object of perception but the person who is perceiving them.[6]

No matter where the inquiry is directed—towards the objects of perception or towards the perceiver—the instruments used in the process are the same, namely, the senses and the mind. The knowledge that is filtered through the senses and the mind is indirect (*parokṣa*)[7]—it is *filtered*, after all. It's not the same as the original. It's changed somehow, perhaps in significant ways.

Most of the knowledge we acquire is indirect. Even the knowledge from books which are believed to be revealed scriptures—such as the Vedas, the Bible, the Qur'an—is indirect.[8] The knowledge acquired via the internet (thank you, Google) is indirect too, as is the knowledge gathered from conversations with friends or from lectures and classes. Come to think of it, the knowledge we acquire through all of these sources is better described as "information"—information about everything that's out there. To the extent it makes us think and reorganize our thoughts in the mind, all such information may lead to knowledge, but it is indirect knowledge nonetheless.[9]

There is no end to the knowledge which concerns the objects of our experience. This world has innumerable

living and nonliving objects of mind-boggling varieties
in size and shape and color and quality. No wonder the
knowledge of the world appears to be inexhaustible.
Empirical sciences deal with this kind of knowledge
admirably well. Every door that science opens through
its breakthroughs reveals another door waiting to be
opened. Every mystery that is solved reveals more
mysteries that need solving.

The knowledge of the world seems doomed to remain
incomplete. It can be endlessly stimulating and no one
doubts that it is enormously fascinating and useful.
What no thoughtful person can honestly deny is that
knowledge of the world is incapable of bringing total
and lasting fulfillment. At least it hasn't done so yet[10]—
which is why it is called "lower knowledge" (*aparā
vidyā*).[11]

Since all of our current knowledge seems to be "lower,"
it is not unreasonable to ask, what kind of knowledge is
"higher"? The answer is, first, higher knowledge (*parā
vidyā*) does not merely inform, it *reveals* the highest
truth.[12] Second—and this is even more important—
higher knowledge totally bypasses the senses and the
mind, which is why it is direct (*aparokṣa*) and pristinely
pure. It reveals reality as it truly is. Higher knowledge
does not concern the world. It concerns the *knower* of
the world. Knowing the world occurs through lower
knowledge. Knowing the knower occurs through higher
knowledge.

Those who have tried to acquire the knowledge of the knower find it to be infinitely more fascinating than the knowledge of the world. Not many seem inclined to do so, it is true, since it is considerably more easy to look out than to look in. The natural inclination of the mind and the senses is to go out. It needs tremendous will-power to take a U-turn: to stop looking at the world for a change and start looking into the heart.[13]

No matter how challenging the process of looking inward is, those who persevere find their efforts generously rewarded with peace, joy and freedom of a magnitude they had never experienced before. Their testimony has proved beyond doubt that the quest for higher knowledge leads to total and lasting fulfillment when the knower is known.

WHO IS THE KNOWER?

In order to figure out who the knower is, we need to recognize that all through life we are almost always dealing with three entities: subject (who initiates action), object (on which the action is focused), and the action itself which connects the two. For instance, if I see a tree, then I am the subject, the tree is the object, and seeing connects me with the tree. If you are reading this book (of course you are!), then you are the subject, the book is the object, and reading connects you with this book.

If the action deals with knowledge (*jñāna*), then the three entities are (1) the subject, who is the knower (*jñātā*), (2)

the object which is to be known (*jñeya*), and (3) the
process of acquiring knowledge, which connects the
knower with the known. It is the knower who is of
special interest in the study of jñāna yoga.

Who is the knower? A short answer to that is "I am."
Knowing is a very personal activity. No one can do it on
my behalf. If I want to know something, I must be the
knower myself. Which means, the only knower I really
and directly know is me. It is for this reason that jñāna
yoga focuses more on the subject than the object. While
the objects towards whom my actions are directed can
be varied, the subject is always me. Who am I? What is
the image that comes before me if I close my eyes and
say "I" a few times? It is almost always the picture of my
body.[14]

The body is the visible and the most obvious part of
who I am. If I want to see how I look, I stand before a
mirror. What I see in the mirror is not me, it's only my
reflection. Maybe not even that, for it is really the
reflection of my body. But I feel that it's a good enough
representation of me. Which is why if the body is fat, I
feel I am fat. If the body is short, I feel I am short. If the
body is in pain, it's me who is in pain. If the body is
male, I identify myself as a male. The body is clearly
who I feel I am. Why else would I celebrate every year
the day this body was born as *my* birthday?

But it is also clear that there is more to me than just the
body. There are other things in me that don't belong to
my body. There are things that no surgeon would find

when my body is cut open. Since these things are invisible, let me just call them collectively the "invisible me." It is not easy to define what this invisible part of me is, but it is enough to recognize that it does the kind of stuff the body cannot do.

Among the things the invisible part accomplishes is thinking, feeling and willing. It seems like there is a repository somewhere within me which contains my thoughts and memories and hopes and fears. There is also something in me which pushes me to do certain things and pulls me away from doing certain other things.

The visible me is the body, which gets things done. The invisible me—let me just call it "mind" for convenience —is the internal instrument which gets certain other things done. Vedanta's term for the mind is the "inner instrument" (*antahkaraṇa*), the implication being that the body is the outer instrument. The choice of the word "instrument" is deliberate. When the body and the mind are referred to as instruments, the obvious question is: who is wielding these instruments? This is another way of asking: am I simply this body and this mind—or is there something else in my "me" besides the body and the mind?

Vedanta's answer to this question is unequivocal. There is indeed something else besides the body and the mind. This something can neither be seen (like the body) nor sensed (like happiness, hope, fear and thoughts in the mind), and yet it is the most significant part of me. This "something else" is not physical. In other words, it is not made up of material particles.

That the body is material is obvious. It is well known that almost 99% of the mass of the human body is made up of six elements: oxygen, carbon, hydrogen, nitrogen, calcium, and phosphorus. The remaining is composed of elements such as potassium, sulfur, sodium, chlorine, fluorine, and magnesium. It is no secret that after death the body is eventually reduced to a heap of dust or ashes when buried or cremated.

What about the mind—is it material or not? There are people for whom the "mind" is nothing more and nothing less than the neurological activity in the brain. There are others, though, who hesitate to conflate mind with brain. They argue that the mind is not the same as the brain, and may be closer to the spirit than the body. According to Vedanta, the mind *is* material but it is different from the brain. The material which makes up the mind is subtle—a whole lot *more* subtle than the material which makes up the human brain.

If we look deeply, we will discover that there is not much difference between the body and the mind. Yes, it's true that we can see the body and not the mind, but that's about it. This difference doesn't really mean much. We don't see an isolated electron either, but that doesn't lead us to conclude that an electron is not a part of the material world. While the body is visible and the mind isn't, in every other way the two are identical.[15] The body needs nourishment, so does the mind. The body can get tired, so does the mind. Both need rest and both are nourished by food. If the body is filled with junk food, it falls sick; so does the mind when filled with junk ideas. The body has its doctors, so does the mind.

Whatever can happen to the body can happen to the mind also. Not only is there a remarkable similarity in them, but they also interact with each other and influence each other, which is why a great many of the illnesses are psychosomatic in nature. Today we are in a position to affirm that the fields of physiology and psychology are not as wide apart as was once thought. They are not identical obviously, but they are interconnected in all sorts of ways. It is possible, perhaps inevitable, to conclude that both body and mind not only are material but are also connected.[16]

The body's materiality is never in question, but there is sometimes resistance to viewing the mind as material, perhaps because the word "spiritual" has been bandied about too often in relation to the mind. It is not unusual to hear people invoking the word "spiritual" when they experience a deep calmness or see a beautiful sunset or read an uplifting poem or hear a stirring song. Every fleeting feeling of wellbeing, which is usually nothing more than a relaxed state of body and mind, gets mistaken for a spiritual experience.

When any and every kind of inspiration is characterized as spiritual, it becomes difficult to look upon the mind as material. But the mind, like the body, follows the laws of matter—and it wouldn't if it weren't material. All that we can surmise is that the mind is very likely composed of very subtle matter, subtler than even the smallest subatomic particle science has been able to discover so far. That, at any rate, is the Vedanta view.

The only nonmaterial part of me, which is distinct from the body and the mind, is the spirit. In Sanskrit, it is called the Ātman, which simply means the self.

THE ĀTMAN

If the nonmaterial part of me is the Ātman, which means self or "me," then are the material parts—body and mind—not me? The question sounds ludicrous. What may not appear so ludicrous is that my present "me" has three parts—the visible me (body), the invisible me (mind), and possibly the spiritual me, or the Ātman.

While some may find this kind of analysis interesting, we cannot ignore the fact that none of us feels like merely being a collection of "parts". We are more than the sum of our parts. A human being is not simply bones, blood, flesh, and thoughts, feelings, hopes, fears, anxieties, and of course the ego—all stacked together inside a form we call the body. We are not a jumble of things piled together. All of these "parts" are organically integrated, somehow giving us that sense of wholeness. Every one of us feels like a complete, undivided person.

All three—body, mind, and the Ātman—somehow seem to work together to make me who I am—or, at least, who I *think* I am. The body and mind, as we have seen, are material and they grow, they change, they evolve. The Ātman is nonmaterial: it doesn't grow, doesn't change and doesn't evolve. Whereas the body and mind are ravaged by time, the Ātman is timeless.[17] It remains the same always. The body and mind keep changing but the Ātman does not.[18]

And yet it is this growing, changing, evolving body/mind combine with which we are most identified. The body and the mind make their presence felt all the time. Almost all of our energy is spent in catering to their constant demands. What is significant here is that we don't generally see their demands as *their* demands. We see them as *our* needs. The body and mind are not "they," they are me. They are myself. Or are they? Are they really my "self"?

Vedanta's answer is an emphatic no. The body and mind are not me. I may have gotten used to referring to them as myself, but they really are not my "self." The Ātman is myself, my *real* self. The body and the mind function *as if* they are the self, but they really aren't. The real me is the Ātman. The Ātman is not just a concept or an idea. The Ātman is not the result of speculation or hope. The Ātman exists. It is real—more real than the body and mind. At present my "me" is a mixture of the *really* real Ātman and only *apparently* real body and mind.

This is a good place to pause and ponder over the meaning of the term "real." Vedanta's definition is a simple equation: real (*sat* or *satya*) = eternal (*nitya*). If something is real, it is eternal and unchanging. Which means that there is no such thing as a temporary reality. If something is real for only a limited time or only under specific conditions, then it is better described as an illusion or a dream. Whatever is really real—not simply "temporarily" real—exists for ever and can never be eclipsed. Whatever changes or disappears periodically or permanently may be an apparition but it's not really real.

With this understanding of what being "real" means, we are in a better position to know who the Ātman is. The Ātman is the real part of me: it cannot be perceived by the senses, but it's never absent. It always is and it never changes. My body and mind can be perceived by me: the body, visually; the mind, through its activity. But both body and mind change with age and disappear from my view occasionally—for instance, in sleep—so body and mind cannot be *really* real.

Where do the body, mind, and Ātman stand in relation to one another? There are at least two ways of conceiving their relationship. In Vedanta texts, the Ātman is sometimes referred to as "master"[19] and sometimes as an "indweller" (*dehī*).[20] When the Ātman is viewed as the master, the body and the mind become the Ātman's instruments (*karaṇa*). An ancient analogy presents the Ātman as the master of a chariot, the intellect as the charioteer, the senses as horses, the mind as the rein, and sense objects as the road on which the chariot is being driven.[21] When the Ātman is viewed as the indweller, the body and the mind become layers or coverings (*kośa*). The Ātman lies hidden under these layers, which are conceived to be either threefold or fivefold, depending on how you catalogue them.

In Sanskrit, each of the threefold layers is called *śarīra*, which literally means "that which wears away," indicating that all of these layers perish sooner or later. The three layers are: gross layer (*sthūla śarīra*), subtle layer (*sūkṣma śarīra*), and causal layer (*kāraṇa śarīra*). The gross layer is what we call the body. The subtle layer, sometimes called the subtle body, comprises the finer and invisible parts of our personality, which include the mind, the intellect, the ego, alongside our feelings, thoughts, ideas and what have you. The causal layer is ignorance (*avidyā* or *ajñāna*). I shall have more to say about ignorance in the next chapter.

When the self is viewed as covered by five layers, the layers have different names: the sustained-by-food self (*annamaya-ātmān*), the filled-with-life self (*prāṇamaya-Ātman*), the mental self (*manomaya-Ātman*), the knowledgeable self (*vijñānamaya-Ātman*), and the blissful self (*ānandamaya-Ātman*).[22] Why is each of these layers called a "self"? Not because the layer is really the self, of course, but because it appears to be so and acts like one until another "self" is discovered within it. When that happens, the outer self's mask falls off and it is revealed to be only a covering. In this way, every subsequent discovery of a self reveals the outer pretending self to be nothing more than a covering, and the process continues until all the layers are peeled off and the true self—the Ātman—is reached.[23]

What is the nature of the Ātman? Granted that it's not material. But that's only saying what it is not, not what it is. If we must give it a name, "consciousness" probably describes it best.

CONSCIOUSNESS

The word "consciousness" doesn't ring the same bell in every mind. Those with a materialistic worldview describe consciousness in material terms. They view it as a result of neurological activity. It is the brain, according to them, which produces consciousness. Every living being is conscious. Life and consciousness go together. When my brain stops working, consciousness ends, life ends, I end. End of story.[24] There is no epilogue, no sequel. Nothing survives. This is the materialistic approach.

Those with a Vedantic worldview don't subscribe to the neuro-reductionist account of the materialists. According to Vedanta, I am not simply a conscious being; my being itself is consciousness. In other words, consciousness is not what I *have*; consciousness is who I *am*. I continue to exist even when the heart stops and the brain dies. Consciousness is not simply a biological process supported by the brain. Consciousness cannot be pigeonholed into the space-time-causation framework.[25] Which means, consciousness doesn't occupy space, it is not ravaged by time, and it is neither the cause nor the effect of anything. All of this means that consciousness is infinite in every way—

undivided by time and space and unrestricted by natural laws.

An object is generally present or implied whenever the word "consciousness" is invoked. We speak of having consciousness (or being conscious) *of* something or someone. It is the consciousness of an object which shows up in the form of neurological activity in the brain. Does the brain produce consciousness—or is it consciousness that triggers brain activity? According to some, it is former; according to Vedanta, it is latter. There is no meeting point between the two so far.[26]

Is there any evidence to prove that the brain produces consciousness? What do we make of the claim that there is no such thing as "mind" apart from the brain?[27] Every scientific experiment on consciousness points to the co-occurrence of mental activity (such as perceiving objects with the help of the senses) with brain activity. But co-occurrence proves neither identity nor causality. At best, the brain is the mind's physiological counterpart, the two may be related but are by no means identical.

Even when we try to connect what happens inside the brain with the awareness of what is sensed outside the body, there is no way to know which of the two caused the other. It is possible to alter a person's mental state through brain stimulation, drugs and surgery, but it is also possible to alter a person's brain activity by asking her to imagine something or direct her attention in a specific way. The cause and effect relationship is far from obvious.[28]

No one can deny that consciousness reveals the presence of objects. Of course it does. Vedanta's position is that consciousness can also stand on its own. Consciousness does not *need* an object. The adjective "pure" is sometimes used to distinguish such objectless consciousness from the consciousness of objects. The analogy of light might help. Light doesn't depend on the objects it illuminates. Light can exist even if there are no objects around. But we know there is light in a room not by seeing the light—no one can *see* light—but only by seeing the illuminated objects in the room. Consciousness is similar. We are aware of its existence because we are conscious of the objects around us, but we haven't become conscious of consciousness itself—yet.

The Ātman is consciousness itself.[29] Without it we wouldn't be conscious of anything. The Ātman is the source of all knowledge. There is nothing we know more intimately and directly than the Ātman.[30] It is in and through the Ātman that everything else is known.[31] And this is why consciousness is first and foremost self-consciousness. When I say, "this is a tree," what I am really affirming is: "*I am conscious that* this is a tree." I wouldn't see a tree unless I was conscious of it. I would perceive nothing if I were not conscious. When we begin to think carefully, we recognize that every experience is possible only because it is powered by the light of consciousness. No consciousness, no experience. It's that simple.

The experience of both body and mind occurs only when we are conscious of them. We are accustomed to thinking of body and mind as conscious entities, but they are not. They are material entities, not inherently conscious. What makes them *seem* conscious is the Ātman, or pure consciousness, whose light percolates through them.[32] Or through the three (or five) layers in which our present personality can be subdivided. The more external the layer, the less is the manifestation of consciousness.

Hidden beneath these layers is the Ātman, the real me. It was never born and it will never die. It always has been, is, and will be. It is pure and perfect. It is infinite and free. Although I am referring to the Ātman as "it," it's really me. Saying that the Ātman is birthless and deathless is the same as saying that I was never born and I will never die. I am divine, pure and perfect. I am free from all limitations and all weaknesses.

It is not surprising that, buried beneath the layers of body and mind, the real me remains hidden from others. What *is* astonishing is how and why the real me is hidden even from me! I should have been the first person to know me, but I am not. Why is it that I see all these layers as "me" while remaining supremely unaware of the *real* me? Why is it that I see the characteristics of the body and mind as *my* characteristics—their limitations as *my* limitations? Why am I not being my true self? Why can't I just be me?

I'm conscious, but I have no experience of being consciousness itself. The Ātman is infinite and free, but I don't feel myself to be infinite and free, certainly not birthless and deathless, and far from being pure and blissful. I don't feel I am divine even though that's who I am. I have no doubt that I am a human being even though that's who I am not. It feels natural to be human and sometimes shocking to be told that I am divine. If I am really the Ātman, then why do I feel I'm a mortal human being, at times happy, sometimes disgruntled, and often miserable?

Vedanta has a simple answer to this question, a one-word key to unlock the door—"ignorance." That is what we turn to now in the following chapter.

IGNORANCE

*E*very time we feel we don't know something, we acknowledge the presence of ignorance. Since we don't know many things—not to speak of the infinite number of things we don't know that we don't know— ignorance is a familiar territory. And yet, like knowledge, ignorance is easy to identify and difficult to define.

Like knowledge, again, ignorance can also be understood in terms of pigeonholing. The mind compares a fresh impression with its stock of past impressions and, when it cannot find a match, it feels lost. It has no idea what the new impression represents, since it is unable to find a box in which to file it. Think of being in a tunnel with no end in sight and hence no light. This is what ignorance feels like. While this is not exactly a definition, it is at least an experience that we are familiar with when we encounter things we know nothing about.

The experience of ignorance is the exact opposite of the experience of knowledge. If ignorance is a dark tunnel, knowledge is the the light at the end of that tunnel. Ignorance leads to bondage whereas knowledge leads to freedom. Ignorance covers knowledge whereas knowledge removes ignorance. Like light and darkness, knowledge and ignorance cannot coexist. If one is, the other is not.

But is ignorance simply the absence of knowledge? It may seem to be so but it is not. Ignorance is the presence of something difficult to pin down—something which is and yet is not, something which both exists and doesn't exist.[1] I know this makes no sense and it is not meant to. For the time being, let us just say that ignorance is a puzzle. Vedanta acknowledges this mysterious nature of ignorance by assigning a special name to it—māyā, which literally means, "that which is not." More explicitly, "that which *appears to be* but really is not."

MĀYĀ

If we look around carefully, we'll be startled to find things in life that are baffling, illogical, pointless and yet somehow considered "normal." Not for nothing is it said that truth can be stranger than fiction. We often want fiction to be logical, believable and true to real life but, come to think of it, "real life" is anything but logical. If we begin to see the contradictions involved in our lives, we'll be stunned at how unbelievable our lives are.[2]

Consider this. None of us knows what lies in our future. Almost every factor that affects our lives is beyond our control. In spite of the uncertainties involved, we keep planning for the future, dreaming about it, and pinning our hopes on it.[3] Yet we have no plan whatsoever for the one certainty in our lives—our eventual death. We don't even want to think about it, although it's something that can happen anytime and anywhere, perhaps sooner than we imagine. Nothing could be more urgent than preparing for this inevitable event, but we choose to ignore it and are often upset or annoyed, even offended, when someone raises the unpleasant topic.

The hope for a better future trumps the dismay at the lackluster present. We slog tirelessly and fantasize endlessly about wealth, fame, recognition, and prosperity. These may or may not come, and even when they do, they come with their own set of problems, as we see from the lives of those who already have them. Yet we cannot stop ourselves from investing most of our time and energy in a pursuit whose rewards are remote, fleeting, and ultimately futile, since death devours everything in a moment.[4]

There is also the mystifying force of attachment, which makes us helplessly cling to places, things and persons, even those who bring us pain and suffering. No one wants pain and no one wants to suffer. What would we not do to throw the burden off! But we cannot. It's not really love that motivates us, since love itself can never produce pain and suffering. But the idea that it could be something else, not love, is unsettling. The world glorifies attachments as love and people continue to suffer.[5]

We long for freedom and every step of the way we are reminded of how little of it we really have. We want to be happy but every ounce of happiness comes at the cost of anxiety, worry and regret. We seek knowledge but it's never enough: no matter how much we know, there is always something we don't know.[6] We thirst after power, but the more we grab it, the more it corrupts us, leaving us weaker than before. We think we can beat the world at its own game, but the world has the last laugh when it uses us to get its work done and then leaves us depleted and ultimately dead in the end.[7]

We can choose to ignore these contradictions. Indeed, most people do precisely that. But life's true colors are revealed to those who care to pause and think. What they discover is the deeper, underlying paradox of life— and this is what is known as māyā in Vedanta. Māyā is neither a mystery nor an illusion. It is simply a statement of facts.[8] It is the world as it really is but the true colors of which, oddly enough, remain hidden in plain sight.

Māyā is the veil which clouds our understanding and makes the ridiculous look normal.[9] Such is its enormous power that, even when we act out of self-interest, as most people do most of the time, we are really acting *against* our interest. The inherent paradoxes of life and the contradictions in which we are forced to live is māyā. We don't seem to have any choice. There is no way out

—or at least that's how it feels most of the time. Māyā is just too powerful.

THE VEIL

Knowledge is power, but so is ignorance. The power of ignorance acts like a veil. The sun is hidden from half of the earth by the earth itself, and lo and behold, it is night! The earth doesn't extinguish the sun, it merely hides it. Ignorance is the veil that "hides" knowledge in the same way.[10] The power of ignorance to hide, to cover, or to conceal (*āvaraṇa-śakti*) is present in every instance of ignorance.

But ignorance has also another power which manifests when the ignorance is partial, not total. Imagine a room with a coiled rope on its floor. It's late evening but the room is not totally dark. Let's say it is dimly lit: there is enough light to know that something is on the floor but not enough to know what that something is. In such situations, the second power of ignorance springs into action. It is called the power to project (*vikṣepa-śakti*).

How does this projection occur? I enter the semi-lit room and see a snake. I panic, perhaps yell with fright, others rush into the room, someone switches on the light, and I discover a rope where I had seen the snake. Had I known it was a rope, I would not have mistaken it for a snake. It was my ignorance that *concealed* the rope and, in its place, *projected* a snake.

When the veil is opaque, only the power to conceal is activated. But both the powers—to conceal *and* to project—are activated when the veil is translucent, as in the case of the semi-lit room. We know that the insufficient light, or partial darkness, not only hid the reality of the rope but also made it possible to project a pseudo snake.

The snake's reality may have been pseudo, but the snake wasn't totally unreal. A little of the reality showed itself in the snake. How else did I see the snake? The "existence" of the snake I saw was really the existence of the rope percolating through the veil of my ignorance. It's just that it had become distorted: the existence of the rope was showing itself as the existence of the snake. Even when I saw the snake, I was really seeing the rope *but not as rope.* That is the kind of mischief played by partial ignorance. It hides the truth only partially. Had I said, "This is a snake," my words would be partly true and partly false. If we divide the sentence into two: (1) This is some object and (2) the object is a snake, (1) is true and (2) is false.

What can happen objectively to a rope can happen subjectively to my own self. Indeed, that's precisely what has happened. Just as the rope was concealed by semi-darkness and a pseudo snake was projected to take its place, the Ātman has been concealed by the translucent veil of māyā and a pseudo self has taken its place. Just as the existence of the snake really belonged to the rope, my present existence really belongs to the Ātman. Because of my ignorance I saw the rope *but not as rope.* In the same way, I perceive myself *but not as the Ātman.*

My misperception of the rope as snake is not too different from my misperception of the divine being—or Ātman—as a human being. It's just that the former happens objectively and the latter subjectively. You can also imagine it this way. What if the rope had forgotten that it was a rope and had begun to see itself as a snake? In which case, it wouldn't be the darkness outside that hid the rope's true identity from itself but the darkness inside, which is what ignorance is.

When my identity as the Ātman is concealed, a new identity is projected—in your case and mine it happens to be the identity of a human being. Once we start down the slippery slope of ignorance, there is no way to know how it will proceed or where it will end. The powers to conceal and to project are perpetually active and they make sure that our identity is never stable. Since the identity is pseudo anyway, why stick to one? Why not flit from one to another?

We do this all the time. I know who I am now, but my present identity is *concealed* when I fall asleep and in its place a new identity is *projected* in my dreams. The world I encounter at this moment is my waking world—or what we ignorantly call the "real" world. The world my dream-identity encounters is the dream world. My identity as a resident of heaven—if there is a heaven and if I go there—will encounter a heavenly world. It's easy to go on and on like this. Rebirth? Not a problem: a different identity in a different world. Or maybe the same world. What difference would it make? There can be any number of worlds and I can have any number of identities, all of them false and every one of them as dependent on the Ātman as the "snake" is on the existence of the rope.[11]

The kind of world I encounter changes when my identity changes. The awake-me encounters the present world, the dreaming-me encounters the dream world, the celestial-me encounters a heaven, the evil-me encounters a hell.[12] The subject and the object, or the perceiver and the perceived, are dynamically related. Any change in the former affects the latter.[13] The world I see when I rage with anger somehow feels different from the world I see when I am calm and content. It's not altogether unreasonable to question whether there is indeed any objective world completely independent of me.

Independent or not, the present reality is that I see myself as a human being and I see the world, but I don't see the Ātman. It's impossible to be simultaneously aware of both the Ātman me and the human me. No one can see both the rope and the "snake" at the same time. If I see one, the other vanishes. The veil of māyā hides the really real and projects the pseudo real in its place.

But what *is* this veil of māyā? The veil that māyā unfurls is composed of time (*kāla*), space (*deśa*), and causality (*nimitta*).[14] It is through this triad that we see ourselves and also the world. When I think of myself, I see myself occupying space, dwelling in time (I was born some years ago, I will die some years hence), affected by causality (karma, the chain of cause and effect). The same is true when I consider the world. We cannot think of anything which isn't bound by time, which doesn't occupy space, and which isn't either a cause or an effect. Every little thing happens somewhere at some time for some reason. All of our empirical sciences operate within this framework.

The fields of study which insist on things being measurable and quantifiable are sometimes categorized as exact or hard sciences. The humanities, in contrast, are soft sciences. Both of these take for granted the framework of time, space and causality. This is so deeply embedded in our minds that its limitation is seldom questioned.[15] Those who dare to do so are not taken seriously. They are usually dismissed as people of "faith" —in other words, people who make unreasonable claims based on blind belief. When a worldview shaped by secular ideals and material sciences is questioned, the tendency is to either sidestep, patronize, trivialize or condemn the question and sometimes even the questioner.

Vedanta dares to look beyond the limiting perspectives of time, space and causality. You don't need to be a believer to do this. All you need is courage to fearlessly question every assumption, no matter how pervasive it may be. If we live in a world which seems circumscribed by notions of time, space and causality, it isn't wrong to ask whether anything lies beyond it. If our own existence seems limited by the triad, it isn't wrong to wonder whether our understanding may be clouded.

The self we identify with and the world this self perceives are both constrained within the bubble of time, space and causality. According to Vedanta, we'll see reality as it is when we pierce the bubble. The veil must be removed to confront the real. As long as I see myself as a mortal being, occupying space and vulnerable to the law of cause and effect, I am still seeing the "snake." When I know that I am the Ātman —timeless, infinite and free—I will have seen the "rope."

FROM THE ONE TO THE MANY

Refracted through the lenses of time, space and causality, the One looks very different. It's an improbable journey from being spirit to being matter. The descent from timelessness into the world of time means immortality is sacrificed for mortality. The descent into the world of space means infinitude is sacrificed for finiteness. The descent into the world of causality means freedom is sacrificed for servitude to laws.

Life on the other side of the veil is not pretty. Gone is the undivided infinite being, who is now replaced by one among the innumerable little beings in a divided, fractured world. Gone is timeless existence, which is now ruled over by time with its constantly shifting borders of past, present and future. Gone is absolute freedom, which is now chained to the inexorable law of cause and effect.

When the infinite becomes finite—or when the whole becomes a part—the immediate effect is the experience of incompleteness. The infinite being was "complete" (*pūrṇa*); the finite being no longer is. From this point forward, the debilitating descent occurs with alarming speed. The gnawing feeling of being incomplete arouses the intense desire (*kāma*) to be complete. This desire leads to action (*karma*) and—welcome to the world of causality—actions lead to results.

As experience, the results are primarily of two kinds: joy (*sukha*) and sorrow (*duḥkha*). When things go well, we experience joy, which may take many forms, gross and subtle, including excitement, satisfaction, contentment, and fulfillment. When things go awry, we experience sorrow, which also takes any number of forms, including physical pain, frustration, depression, and anger. No matter what forms joy and sorrow take, these can be experienced only through a body and mind—hence the process called birth, which brings a body/mind into being. If we ever wondered why we were born at all, there is a one-word answer to it: *karma*. If we ever wondered why karma entered into the equation, there is another one-word answer to it: *ignorance*.

Even as the joy and sorrow are experienced by the finite being, its relentless struggle to regain completeness continues to produce more karma leading to more of

both joy and sorrow, eventually getting another body
when the present one is worn out and discarded.
Effectively, the finite being is now trapped in a circular
trajectory of karma, birth, and experience. The circle
has no beginning and no end.

Most remain blissfully ignorant of this repetitive and
monotonous structure, but a few become intensely
aware of what's going on. They see through the fleeting
experiences of life and come face to face with a deeper
truth, namely, life in its present form is bereft of real
freedom, joy and fulfillment. Note the word "real": It is
not as if we don't have freedom, joy and fulfillment at
present. We do have them, perhaps not as much as we
want, but still there is no denying their presence in our
lives. Nevertheless, we cannot also deny that our present
freedom, joy and fulfillment are quite fragile: there're
here today, gone tomorrow. What we are saddled with,
in various forms, are pain and frustration caused by
physical and mental limitations.

This completes the descent from the one to the many,
from freedom to bondage, and from bliss to sorrow. Now
there is nowhere else to go and nothing else to do other
than to revolve endlessly in this vicious circle of relative
existence (saṁsāra), which is ephemeral, and yet in a
strange sort of way—it persists! It's like a river that stays
in place even though the water is continually moving.
What keeps the process going is a chain known as the
karma chain.

We have seen the path along which the descent occurs: ignorance → desire → karma → birth → sorrow.

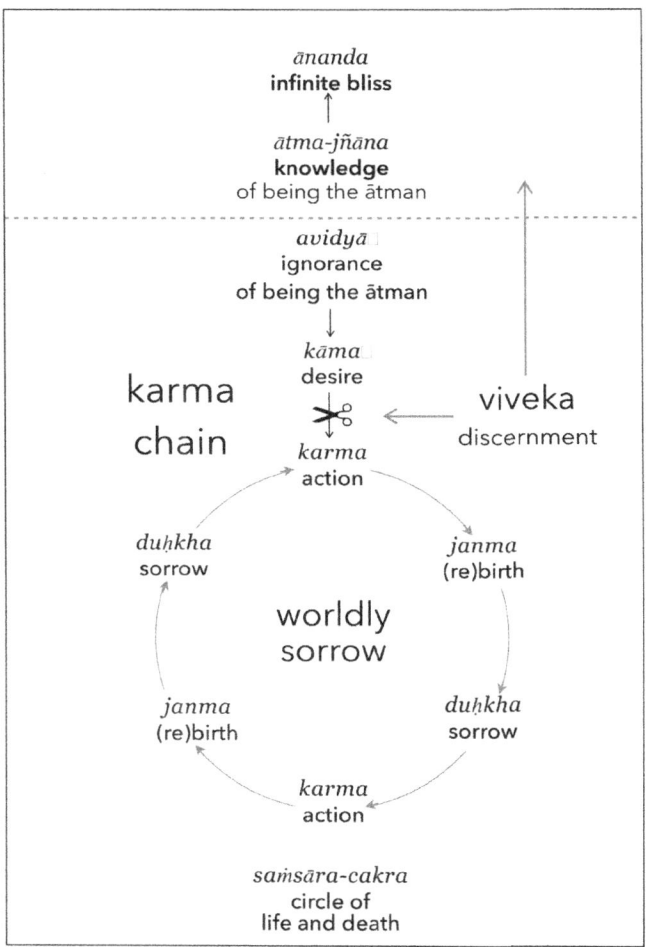

It is ignorance that sets the ball rolling—but no one knows when the ball began to roll. Ignorance has this peculiarity: it's impossible to know when it begins. What we do know is that ignorance ends when knowledge dawns. Since ignorance triggers the karma chain, ignorance is the primal cause. In the threefold covering over the Ātman, ignorance is therefore called the *causal* layer (*kāraṇa śarīra*).

The karma chain eventually forms a loop—karma → birth → sorrow—which repeats endlessly. It is along this loop that the hapless spirit, which is in the thrall of ignorance, keeps revolving. A circular journey means perpetual movement. Like any circle, it has no beginning and no end.

Are we doomed to remain continually moving in this circle? Not really. The only way to get out of this mess is to break the karma chain. Any chain is only as strong as its weakest link. The weakest link of the karma chain is the one that connects desire with karma. The method is to snap this link and break the chain. What distinguishes the four yogas of Swami Vivekananda from one another is the use of a different instrument to break the karma chain. In jñāna yoga, the instrument that snaps the weakest link is discernment (*viveka*).

TO BE AND NOT TO BE

Hamlet's dilemma was to be or not to be. If Hamlet were māyā, he would have embraced a third choice: to be *and* not to be. Logically this option makes no sense, of course. How can something be and not be at the same time? This is not really possible. The keyword is "really."

Is it *un*-really possible to be and not be at the same time? The answer is yes.

Anything is possible so long as it is not real. Not everything that happens in our dreams makes sense from our waking perspective. Things that look normal in dreams seem bizarre when we wake up. Even if what we see in a dream is not bizarre, there is still the problem of being in two places at the same time. I am asleep in my bed (in the "real" world) and, *at the same time*, drinking tea with friends (in my dream world). What makes this possible is that while my sleep seems real, it is easy to dismiss drinking tea with friends in a dream as unreal.

Let's go back to the snake I mistakenly perceived in my semi-lit room. Was that snake real? Of course not. Was that snake unreal? This question is difficult to answer. I can't say the snake was real, but I can't say it was unreal either. If it wasn't there, how did I see it? Why would I panic after seeing an unreal snake which wasn't there? Clearly, when I saw it—and until I realized it was a rope —the snake was real *to me*.

My problem is this: I can't say that the snake was real, I can't say that the snake was unreal, I can't say that the snake was both real and unreal, and I can't say that the snake was neither real nor unreal. Which is rather a longwinded way of saying that I cannot say anything definitively about the status of the snake.[16] Such objects which defy clear categorization into either real (*sat*) or unreal (*asat*) are dumped into a third category called "apparently real" (*mithyā*)—or seemingly real until their unreality is exposed.

Māyā or ignorance belongs to this category.[17] Maya is "apparently real." It exists but not really. Its presence cannot be denied since we see its mischief all around us. Its reality cannot be affirmed since it vanishes with knowledge. Its existence is temporary, like that of a dream. I cannot deny that I saw a dream last night. But I cannot say that the dream world is real just because I saw it, since it disappeared the moment I woke up. Dreams vanish when we wake up physically. Māyā vanishes when we wake up spiritually.

Just as māyā is apparently real, so are its products, the world among them. Human creatures like you and me are also products of māyā. As a human being I am apparently real. But as Ātman I am *really* real. That's how I can be immortal, free and infinite and, *at the same time*, mortal, bound and finite. The former, really; the latter, apparently.[18] As long as I am absorbed into my apparent identity as a human being, I am shut out of my real identity as the Ātman. It's like when I am absorbed into my dream world, I am shut out of the waking world. The only way to end the dream is to wake up.

We do wake up now and then but only for a while, usually only for a few moments at the most, then we fall asleep and resume dreaming. Vedanta teachers narrate the story of a bird feasting on the fruits of a tree. The fruits are delicious and the bird is in bliss until it pecks on an exceptionally bitter fruit. The fruit is so bitter that the bird pauses and almost decides to stop eating. It looks up and, to its amazement, finds on the top of the tree a bird sitting in peace, ignoring the fruits and filled with light.

The lower bird is immediately attracted to it and hops on to a higher branch in an effort to get closer to the other bird. But then it finds more fruit hanging invitingly nearby, forgets the higher bird, and resumes eating—until, yet again, a bitter fruit forces it to stop. It looks up again at the shining bird, hops closer to it, and is once again distracted by fruits. This on-again and off-again upward journey of the bird continues until it comes so close to the higher bird that its effulgence engulfs the lower bird and it makes a startling discovery: there were never really two birds, one higher and the other lower. There was only one bird all along. The lower bird was only a projection, not really real—a silly reflection or a bad dream.[19]

Eating the "fruits" of my karma, both sweet and bitter, and experiencing joy and sorrow is what I am doing now in the "dream" of this world. Detachment comes over me now and then, I sort of "wake up," and see another being—a higher, better self—filled with light, freedom and bliss. I make an effort to let go of my present preoccupations and approach the higher self. I discover a little peace and freedom until I fall asleep again and resume devouring more fruits. I wake up when I bite into another bitter fruit but, soon enough, go to sleep again and the circle keeps revolving.

The practice of jñāna yoga can be seen as a series of awakenings punctuated by periods of dreaming. When the practice matures, the waking periods last longer and the dreams become fewer. The goal is to wake up fully and permanently into the light of knowledge and to discover that the higher self is none other than my own self. Once this knowledge dawns, there is no drowsing off again in the darkness of ignorance.

The key practice which triggers the process of waking up is discernment. A bitter experience sometimes helps in shaking us out of our torpor, but discernment is the primary force which wakes us up and helps us to remain awake. Discernment stays with us until māyā disappears, the veil is removed, and the truth shines bright and clear. Discernment is the instrument which breaks the karma chain and frees us from the never-ending sorrow-go-round of relative existence. Discernment is what we shall now turn to in the following chapter.

DISCERNMENT

*L*et us go back to that semi-lit room where I saw the "snake." The instinctive fear and the cry for help are perhaps understandable. But soon after the initial reaction, what if I had paused and said to myself, "Isn't it bizarre to see a snake here? There are no snakes in this neighborhood. Let me look a bit more carefully." I could have either peered more closely or switched on the light and seen that the "snake" was really a rope.

The practice of looking carefully and deeply is the practice of discernment (*viveka*). Discernment helps us to see things as they truly are. Discernment is the key discipline in jñāna yoga. Those who take things at face value seldom pause to ask questions. Jñāna yoga is not for them. Jñāna yoga is for the curious and the inquisitive. It is for those who are endowed with a healthy dose of skepticism. The practice of *every* yoga needs discernment, but in no yoga more so than in jñāna yoga.

The practice of discernment cannot succeed unless it fulfills some basic requirements. One obvious requirement is a staunch refusal to accept anything without examining it closely. Blind allegiance to any convention is a big no-no. Even conventional wisdom is put to test and nothing is accepted unless and until it is found reasonable.

The method is simple: to keep asking questions. It is the method perfected by the Vedic sages in ancient times and which, centuries later, was employed in Greece by Socrates. Today it's the staple of all scientific inquiry. The practice of discernment requires the ability to ask questions without fear and to elicit answers that are logical and reasonable.

A discerning mind is smart enough to recognize that even reason has its limits and the search cannot be—indeed, *should not be*—stifled by any limits. Reason operates only within the realm of māyā, which is conditioned by time, space and causality. Beyond this realm lies a shoreless expanse, where even the idea of time, space and causality doesn't exist. It is through the Upaniṣads that we get a glimpse into this transcendental reality. This reality cannot be reached via reason but it doesn't contradict reason.[1] To reach there we undertake a journey, but it is not a journey in space and time. It is a journey through material layers, each of which is increasingly subtler, greater and more inward.[2] At the end of this journey, the Ātman is "reached"—which is same as saying that the knower is known.

If the wisdom of the Upaniṣads transcends reason, it doesn't look like the Upaniṣads can be questioned. This is not true. Vedanta has always been open to questions. In fact, it is Vedanta's openness to questions that has made it such a robust philosophy. Over the centuries healthy debates between differing schools of thought have left precious few issues unaddressed and unresolved. Some of the greatest minds of the past and present have grappled with these issues, relentlessly asking questions, raising doubts, and presenting competing worldviews. The ongoing engagement with diverse ways of thinking has made Vedanta not only strong but universal in its outreach.

What is not often recognized is that every question is grounded in certain presuppositions. For instance, every "why" question assumes that everything happens for a reason; every "when" question assumes the existence of time; every "where" question assumes the existence of space; and every "how" question assumes cause-and-effect relationships.[3] None of these questions can be asked if their assumptions themselves are under scrutiny, as they are in jñāna yoga.

This doesn't mean that the Upaniṣads shouldn't be questioned. All that this means is that it's good to be aware that all of our questions are based on a specific worldview and become redundant while examining another worldview with a different set of assumptions. In order to ask meaningful questions in Vedanta, familiarity with its worldview is essential.

A worldview is a "story" that provides a conceptual framework to answer questions and to interpret experiences. Every authentic tradition presents a story— and every story deserves careful examination. It's not necessary to believe in Vedanta's worldview, but we must at least make an effort to understand it. Only then would it be possible to raise questions and express misgivings, if any. At no stage should we surrender the freedom to reject Vedanta if it doesn't meet our standard of truth.

Speaking of truth, just because something is logical doesn't mean that it's true. Vedanta's worldview is logical enough, but that in itself does not make it true. Like every worldview, Vedanta's worldview—or "story" —*points to* what is real. It is only a pointer, not the reality itself. The finger pointing at the moon is not the moon. It is not logical consistency that makes Vedanta authentic but the fact that Vedanta practice has led to snapping the karma chain, eliminating ignorance, and attaining knowledge. In experiential terms, this has resulted in steady, unending bliss unpunctuated by pain and suffering.

All of this has been directly experienced in the past and continues to be experienced even today. It is not

something to be only believed in or accepted on faith.
Which is not to imply that faith has no value whatsoever.
Every undertaking is powered by faith, at least enough
faith to make it worthwhile investing time and energy in
it. Faith is essential to pursue a meaningful project.
What is called for is not a blind allegiance to the
Upaniṣads but the willingness to accept them at least as
a working hypothesis and the determination to practice
what they teach in order to verify their claims through
one's own direct experience.

When faith, which powers the practice, matures into
direct experience, it has served its purpose. Which is why
the study and practice of Vedanta begins with faith but
it shouldn't end there.[4] Faith is the starting point, not an
end in itself. The Upaniṣads must be subjected to the
test of reason, and pursued as far as reason is capable of
pushing the inquiry. The leap beyond the limits of
reason occurs through practice. The final and conclusive
test of any truth, therefore, is that it can be verified
through one's own direct experience.[5]

These, then, are basic requirements for the practice of
discernment: accepting nothing blindly, subjecting
everything to a thorough examination, and fearlessly
asking questions in order to get to the truth. Taken
together, these make discernment a most powerful
practice.

QUESTIONS ABOUT THE WORLD

The world is only a string of sensations to a newborn. There is hardly any meaning associated with those sensations and the baby has no words to express what she feels. Gradually things begin to acquire meaning, words begin to make sense, language skills begin to develop, and then questions arise. What kind of questions are asked depends on age, interest and upbringing. Not everyone asks the same kind of questions and not everyone expects the same kind of answers. The world-related questions of those with a discerning nature may take any or all of the following forms.

What do we really mean by "world"? It is a tricky word: commonly used and diversely employed. In a collective sense, the word is used to refer to everything other than one's own self. Physically it can refer to the extent of the material universe known to cosmologists and astrophysicists. Often the word refers to natural forces and, just as often, to living beings, and usually to human beings. Some have only this planet earth in mind when they speak about the "world."[6]

What most of us imply by "world" most of the time is an entity much smaller. We normally move within a limited geographical area and meet with a relatively small number of people while engaged in a repetitive chore of duties—and it is this bubble in which our life revolves that usually comprises our own little world. On the outer fringes of this world are places and people we have read about or seen online or on TV. We may be reminded of them occasionally while watching the news or reading the papers or while on a trip to a distant place. But by and large our activities, physical and mental, remain confined within the bubble. For all practical purposes it is this bubble that serves as our world.

This world of ours is predominantly self-referential. Only that which is related to me, or to which I can relate in some way, becomes my idea of the "world."[7] Which is why no two people have an identical view of the world.[8] Sometimes the views are so diametrically opposed to one another that we wonder whether they point to the same world. How often have we heard someone say, "This is a terrible world," and someone else say, "How wonderful this world is!" Sometimes these are the words of the same person on different days.[9] We view the world through the lens of the mind: my world is tinted with the color of my mind, your world is tinted with the color of your mind. Since the colors are different and they keep changing, it's no surprise that what we see out there doesn't exactly match.[10]

Is this world real? This might seem to be a strange question to ask, perhaps outrageous, even silly. But a discerning mind needs to ask this question nonetheless. After all, what is the evidence that the world exists? The only evidence we can point to is that we experience the world: we can see it, we can hear it, we can smell it, we can touch it, and we can taste it. Moreover, our mind *feels* it to be real.[11] Unfortunately, this is not enough of a reason to conclude that the world is real, because all of these things happen in dream as well.

But the dream world's reality is out of the question. After all, the dream world doesn't exist before I sleep and it doesn't exist after I wake up. It *seems to* exist only as long as I am dreaming. It's true that it feels real that time but when I wake up and see the "real" world, I know that what I saw in my sleep was only a dream. Unfortunately, again, this is exactly true with regard to our so-called real world as well. It doesn't exist before I wake up and it doesn't exist after I sleep. It *seems to* exist only as long as I am awake.

Or does it? It is tempting to assume that the world continues to exist for others when I am asleep. No harm in making that assumption provided I accept that, in the same way, my dream world continues to exist for others in my dream even after I wake up. Am I willing to concede that? Am I also willing to assume that the dream world existed before I found myself in it? Seriously—does it sound credible that the waking world and all of my dream worlds exist simultaneously and we pop in and out of them periodically?[12]

It would be closer to truth to admit that the dream world exists for me when I am dreaming and the waking world exists for me when I am awake. There is no way for me to definitively confirm or deny that either of these worlds exists when I am not aware of it. This raises a larger and deeper question: am I aware of the world because it is there, or is the world there because I am aware of it?

None of this proves that the world is not real, but it does raise reasonable doubts about it.[13] It is possible to be as dogmatic about the reality of this world as about its unreality. Neither is necessary. All that a discerning mind has to acknowledge is that there is no way to prove that the world is real while we are *in the world,* just as there is no way to prove that the dream is unreal while we are *in the dream.*

We judge a dream to be unreal when we wake up and encounter a reality which somehow feels *more* real than the dream. It is only in comparison with our waking experience that we judge dreams to be unreal. If we choose to perceive levels of reality—we already do this when we judge the world to be *more* real than a dream, which itself had seemed real until we woke up—then we cannot deny that it is possible for something else to be even *more* real than the world.

This is not only a theoretical possibility but also a reality confirmed through experience. There have been people —and there will always be some in every generation— who have experienced something which is more real, more "intense," than this world.[14] When Vivekananda as a young man asked Sri Ramakrishna whether he had seen God, his answer couldn't have expressed the truth in a better way: "Yes, I see God just as I see you here, only in a much intenser sense."[15]

QUESTIONS ABOUT ME

We cannot say anything definitively about the world: Is it real? Is it unreal? Does it exist when I'm not aware of it? There are no clear answers to these questions. The ambiguity makes the world neither helpful nor interesting to a discerning jñāna yogī.[16] What *is* interesting and certainly more helpful to a jñāna yogī is to pay careful attention to one who is experiencing the world—me! After all, it's me who certifies that the world exists, so it makes sense to check out the credentials of the certifying authority.

So, then, who is this "me"? My present "me" is a combination of the visible (the body), the invisible (mind, intellect, ego), and the spiritual (the Ātman): the first two are material and the third is nonmaterial.[17] How the material and the nonmaterial combine into a seamless whole would have been a mystery, except that they don't. Their combination is similar to the "combination" of the rope with the "snake" in a semi-lit room.

Just as the snake "hides" the rope, the material hides the spiritual. The rope and the snake cannot be seen at the same time: when I see one, I don't see the other. In the same way, the material me and the spiritual me don't meet each other: when I am identified with one, I get disconnected from the other.[18] And yet—and this is the mysterious part—they *seem* to coexist. When they do, it seems *as if* the material covers the spiritual and *as if* the spiritual remains hidden within. This impossible feat is made seemingly possible by māyā, the power which controls us until we know it doesn't.

Which of the two me's—material and spiritual—is the real *me?* If a thing is real, it must be eternal. Temporary or time-bound reality is a euphemism for a dream or a hallucination—in other words, a misperception. A simple test to find the real me is to check whether it ever disappears. If it does, it's not me. The real me—if it is *really* real—should be always present, no matter what, since real = eternal. This is not true of the body: it disappears when I fall asleep. I am no longer conscious of my sleeping body. I may run and dance in my dreams, but the body that does it is not the same as the one sleeping in my bed.

The activity of the mind manifests in sleep as a dream and it creates a world not essentially different from the one we normally treat as real. But the mind also disappears in deep sleep, when dreams cease. I am conscious of neither the body nor the mind in deep sleep. The disappearance of both body and mind may be temporary, but that disqualifies them from being

considered "real." They are not real and they are
not me.

What never disappears but remains constant is the
consciousness of waking, dream and deep sleep. If I
weren't conscious of these states, I wouldn't even
experience them. I am conscious when I am awake (at
this very moment, as I write this, for instance); I am
conscious when I am dreaming (I couldn't see the dream
unless I were conscious of it, could I?); I am conscious
when I am in deep sleep (which is how I remember the
following morning my experience of it: "I had a blissful
sleep. I wasn't aware of anything else!"). The Ātman is
the consciousness which unifies the experience of all the
three states. It is the Ātman which is the real me. Or, to
put it simply, bluntly, and accurately: *I am the Ātman.*

I am the Ātman? Isn't "I" the ego? The answer is yes to both
the questions. If that sounds contradictory, it is because
the self is being confused with the sense of "I". It is
through discernment that I realize that I am not the "I."
How am I different from my "I"?

The "I", or ego, provides me with an "I" sense. It
separates me from whatever it determines is "not me"—
and this "not me" becomes my "world." The "not me"
—or "the other"—makes relationships possible. "The
other" may be a person, a place, an object, and idea, or
whatever. Some of these I may want to either possess or
run away from. Once a want is created, the desire to
fulfill it arises, and it forces me to do something about it.

Which is how the ego makes me think of myself as a doer: I do karma. It also makes me think of myself as the experiencer: I experience the results of karma. When my desire is fulfilled I feel happy; when it is not, I feel miserable. In this way the ego keeps me tied to the karma chain.

The Ātman couldn't be more different from the ego. The Ātman is neither the doer nor the experiencer. Karma has no sway over the Ātman. Moreover, the Ātman shatters the barriers that separate me from others, living and nonliving. The idea of "I and mine" is absent in the Ātman. It's the material me that is separate from the material world: *my* body, *my* mind, *my* ideas, *my* hopes—all of these can be distinguished from those of others.

But the nonmaterial me, or the Ātman, has no boundaries. My Ātman is not different from your Ātman. You and I seem to be different, it is true, but that is because we are identified with "I"-s attached to different bodies and minds. Once the "I" is out of the way, there is no way to distinguish one Ātman from another. It's like two waves: once they subside, there is no way to distinguish one from the other.

The wave identity is temporary. When a wave subsides, it's not dead and gone. What is a wave other than some water of the ocean shaped into a specific form and moving in a specific way? As a wave, it has a distinct identity. Once its wave identity ends, it doesn't stop existing. It simply goes back to being one with the

ocean.[19] As a human being, I am a wave. As the Ātman
I am the ocean. The Ātman unifies everything into an
undivided whole. The Ātman is all that there is.[20]

When all material vestiges are shed, I stand alone and
infinite. There is no sense of "I" there, first, because
there is no *there* there and, second, because there is no
"world" from which I need to distinguish myself. When
everyone and everything is me, and there is neither you
nor this nor that anywhere anytime, even the *idea* of
"me" becomes meaningless. When māyā is declawed,
the ego disappears and, along with it, my identity as a
finite, mortal creature. I become infinite and immortal,
filled with joy, perfection and freedom.

That experience seems far off at present, because the
Ātman is in the clutches of māyā and is "covered" with
material layers which endow it with an "I" attached to a
body and mind which become "me." Of course, the
Ātman is only deluded into thinking that it is under
māyā's control. The Ātman's bondage is not real. The
"snake" in the semi-lit room was not real either, but that
didn't stop me from being terrified. Such is māyā's
mesmerizing magic that the Ātman's innate freedom
and joy don't stop it from experiencing bondage and
suffering.[21]

QUESTIONS ABOUT GOD

You and I and every embodied creature is the
"suffering" Ātman. It is the pain of suffering which
forces us to find ways to overcome it. While there are

quick fixes available, none of them seems to root out the problem completely. One ancient and time-tested way to get a permanent fix to the problem of suffering is to seek God's help.[22] Not everyone does this, of course, but some of us do. When a discerning mind begins to think of God, it is natural for questions to arise. Any number of questions are possible. Beginning with the obvious:

Who is God? One possible answer: God is one from whom everything originates, on whose support everything depends, and to whom everything returns.[23] This bare-bones answer accounts for not only the presence of the world but also how it is supported and where it ends up. What the answer doesn't explain is how everything originates from God, what God's support really means, and what going back to God entails—and, most importantly, who God really is without reference to you, me and the world.

There hasn't yet been a universally acceptable explanation, and almost certainly there never will be. Has there been *anything* at all which is acceptable to everyone, everywhere? What we do have instead are several different answers provided at different points in history by different people from different parts of the world, which is how different religious traditions have emerged.

It's no surprise that the answers are different. What to speak of speculations, even answers backed by a revelation or direct experience of God are bound to be

different. When an experience is clothed in words
using language and culture-specific symbols, metaphors
and imagery, it is bound to have a distinct texture and
color. What is important to acknowledge is that, in
spite of the answers that sometimes look radically
different from one another, they represent sincere
human efforts to understand and describe God. The
efforts are never fully successful, but that is only to be
expected. After all, how can you ask for a perfect
description of a transcendent being who is essentially
indescribable?

Does God exist? Faced with multiple answers about God's
identity, each claiming to be right and none uncontested,
it is natural to wonder if God really exists or is only a
"belief," a nebulous entity who can be propped up only
on the strength of faith. Some affirm that God exists,
but their subjective experience cannot be objectively
proved. Others seem too confident that God doesn't
exist, although their assertion is as much a statement of
faith as of those who feel that God *does* exist. A few
others claim that no one knows—and no one can *ever*
know—whether God exists. One is left with the feeling
that both atheism and agnosticism have today become
religions of sorts.

According to Vedanta, God not only exists but is
existence itself. This means, claiming that God doesn't
exist is tantamount to saying, "Existence doesn't exist."
Funnily enough, this brings into question even the

existence of the person who claims that God doesn't
exist.

It is significant that the teaching of God as existence (*sat*)
is not laid down as a dogma or an article of faith. It is
simply a revelation found in the Upaniṣads. Everyone is
welcome to study what it means, to examine it carefully,
to ask questions about it, and to confirm whether it fits
well in the Vedantic worldview. If God as existence
resonates with our own orientation to the divine, its
truth can be verified through personal experience.

Vedanta goes a step further: God not only is existence
itself but God alone exists. There *is* nothing else apart
from God. If something else appears to exist, that too is
nothing but God.[24] The word for God that is commonly
used in Vedanta is "Brahman." Brahman is neither a
person nor a power nor anything that can be described
through words. Literally, "Brahman" simply means the
vast, the infinite—which is how existence itself is. What
we can say with absolute certainty is this: God *is*. Any
description we add after "is" may be helpful, but it also
somehow circumscribes God's infinitude and
compromises God's ineffability.

Which means, even "God is existence itself" is not a
perfect description. What it really implies is that God is
not nonexistence (*asat*). In other words, God is not unreal.
Likewise, when God is viewed as pure consciousness (*cit*
or *caitanya*), what is really implied is that God is *not*
material (*jaḍa*). When God is viewed as infinite (*ananta*),
what is really implied is that God is *not* finite or mortal

(*martya*). Put simply, if we want an accurate description of God, we can only say what God is not, never what God is. After eliminating everything that God is not, whoever remains is God.

If it is God we turn to in times of difficulty, it is reasonable to ask: *how can I receive help from an indescribable God about whom I know nothing?* The answer is this: when there is a need, God becomes the fulfiller of the need and no longer remains indescribable. God *becomes* a helper-God when the Ātman *becomes* a being in need of help. God simply *is* as long as I simply *am.* The moment I become a seeker, for me God becomes the sought. When I become a child, God becomes my father or my mother. When I feel lost, God becomes my guide. When I need company, God becomes my friend. When I am in trouble, I need someone to rescue me. The prayers of the "troubled" Ātman are answered by the "troubleshooter" God.

As we have seen already, the subject and the object are dynamically related: when the subject changes, so does the object. God's *becoming* someone else is as real—more accurately, as "apparently real"—as the Ātman's *becoming* someone else. The water next to my bed is of no use when I am thirsty in my dream. Only dream-water can quench my dream-thirst. In order for me to receive God's help, the God I turn to must belong to the same level of reality as mine. When the Ātman is apparently transformed, there is also an apparent transformation in the God whom the Ātman worships and adores.

God thus takes many forms. When the Ātman becomes an individual self (*jīvātman*), God becomes the supreme self (*paramātman*). When the Ātman becomes a devotee (*bhakta*), God becomes one endowed with divine qualities (*bhagavān*). When the Ātman becomes a creature, God becomes the creator. When the Ātman becomes a resident of God's kingdom, God becomes the ruler (*īśvara*) or the supreme ruler (*parameśvara*).[25]

When the Ātman stops becoming anything, so does God. That's the moment the duality ends.[26] Since it never really existed, duality's end is as apparent as its existence.[27] God alone continues to exist, the way God always has. Which is same as saying that the Ātman alone continues to exist, the way it always has. Both these statements are not only accurate but identical, because Brahman and Ātman are one and the same reality.[28] When the reality is viewed with reference to an individual, it is Ātman. When the same reality is viewed with reference to no one in particular, it is Brahman, or God, who is beyond all names, forms and concepts.[29]

Religion can be viewed as a dynamic relationship between the apparently changed Ātman and the apparently changed God.[30] The goal of religion is reached when this relationship reaches its culmination with the realization of total identity: the "sleeping" Ātman wakes up and the dream vanishes.[31] The boundaries that separated the Ātman from God and from everything else evaporate. Forms disappear, names disappear, limitations disappear. What remains is the truth—call it Ātman or Brahman or by any other name or by no name at all. Who cares? What's in a name anyway?

All of this can be confusing. God is said to be indescribable and yet descriptions of God abound in religious texts. God is said to be one and yet I see people worshiping a God who seems to be different from my own. *How do I make sense of all this?* The first thing to remember is that none of God's descriptions is perfect. An imperfect description is nevertheless better than no description, since that's about the best we can do, considering our limited expressing skills and the inherent limitation of language. However imperfect God's description may be, it still gives us enough idea to make a beginning in spiritual life.

The second thing to remember is that, all said and done, our descriptions of God, our explanations of who God is, are all "human" explanations. This is unavoidable. Our all-too-human minds are trying to make sense of the world, its origin and its purpose. We cannot but see everything from the human perspective. No wonder we tend to put human beings on top of the evolutionary ladder and look at everyone else as somehow inferior or at least less capable. A dog or a cat may have different ideas. Who knows what animals think of us and what *their* ideas of God are![32]

The third thing to remember is that we human beings
don't have an idea of God on which we all agree. This is
because our minds don't think in an identical manner.
Nevertheless, none of the ways in which a sincere
struggling soul thinks of God is wrong. The God I
worship is the God I need in my present state of
evolution. As I evolve, my concept of God evolves too.[33]
At every stage, God responds to me in a way that is
appropriate in our relationship and in a way that helps
my evolution. So every way in which God is approached
deserves respect, since they all represent ways to reach
the same divine being. Every one of us is unique in our
own way, so the divine we worship is also unique for us
on our own mental horizon. God is one. Our
perceptions of God are many.[34]

In the beginning, God may appear to be a being far
removed from me, staying in a distant place and
controlling the universe like a governor, rewarding the
good and punishing the wicked. Over time, when my
ideas evolve and my love overcomes fear, God becomes
a benign figure and comes closer to me. The love that
connects me with God makes me feel that I belong to
God: if God is the whole, I am a part of that whole.
Such is the power of love that it slowly absorbs and
engulfs everything. My love for God may reach a point
when I no longer feel I am merely connected with God.
The awareness of my separate identity becomes a
burden at that stage—the two identities merge and all
distinctions vanish. The journey often begins with
dualism, passes through the intermediate stage of

qualified nondualism, and finally ends with
nondualism.[35]

WEIGHING MY OPTIONS

Let us review what discernment has taught us about the
world, the self and God. First, the world. No matter
how real the world seems, it is difficult to determine
whether the world is *really* real, considering how similar
it is to the world experienced in dreams.[36] Life as we
know it may well be nothing more than an endless series
of dreams, one following another.[37] The waking dream
followed by dream-dream which, in turn, is followed by
deep sleep-dream—three kinds of dreams in a 24-hour
cycle.[38]

After a dream-event called death, we may have a
heaven-dream or a hell-dream, or a dream of being in
some other celestial world or perhaps a dream of being
reborn in this world. These dreams keep changing and
keep going on and on and on. In every dream I have a
different persona but the same experience of stress and
anxiety, pain and suffering, disease and death. None of
this will end unless and until I wake up. When I do, I
will know at last who I am, who I always was, and who I
will always be.[39]

The study of Vedanta helps. It points me to a deeper,
truer core, the *real* me, compared to which all other parts
of my personality are, at best, only coverings. The real
me is pure and perfect, infinite and blissful. The
puzzling part is that I presently find myself enmeshed in

a world which I don't understand and with no knowledge of how I got here. Even more troubling is the discovery that the coverings over me have become indistinguishable from me. All of this has hidden me from myself, resulting in lack of freedom. Through discernment I recognize that my suffering is tied up with my ignorance of who I am. With my true identity forgotten, I have now begun to see myself as a mortal, weak, human being.

Seeking help, I look up to an immortal, strong, divine being—God. Vedanta identifies God with existence (*sat*), consciousness (*cit*) and bliss (*ānanda*).[40] Through discernment I am able to see that my concept of God evolves as I evolve. The God I worship is the God I need. As my needs change and evolve, the way I see God changes and evolves as well. With increasing clarity of mind and purity of heart, my *relationship* with God gradually matures into *identity* with God—it is then that I regain my apparently lost freedom, perfection and bliss.

At present, though, my experience couldn't be more different: I feel the bondage intensely, I know I am far from perfect, and I'm nowhere near the eventual bliss that is to come. What are my options? There are two: an easy option and a challenging option. The easy option is to do nothing different, maintain the status quo and do what most people do, which is to continue stumbling on life's shifting terrain with its ups and downs, hoping against hope that all will be well someday somewhere. If this is the option you choose, go ahead and put this book down now. There is no need to ever pick it up again.

The rest of the book is for those who have the grit and the courage to choose the other option, the challenging option. This option is meant for those who are not afraid of change and are willing to do whatever it takes to find the truth.[41] This is not easy, but it won't appear impossible if the effort is backed by patience, perseverance and sincerity. Read on only if this is the option you choose.

What *is* this challenging option? This option is to fearlessly address the root cause of the problem. We have already discerned that the cause is ignorance, which has set in motion a karma chain that has tied me to an unfulfilling life and robbed me of my freedom. We have also seen that the weakest link of the chain is the one connecting desire with karma. The challenge is to strike hard at this link and break the vicious chain. Only then will I be free, *really* free. Only then can suffering end for ever.

All of the yogas are capable of demolishing the nefarious link between desire and karma and every yoga uses a different instrument to do so. In bhakti yoga, the primary instrument used is intense love and longing. In karma yoga, the instrument is detachment. In raja yoga, the instrument is inner discipline. In jñāna yoga, the subject of our present study, the primary instrument used to snap the link is discernment.

DISCERNMENT AND DESIRE

We have seen that desire is the direct result of ignorance. In order for me to want anything, I must either know that I lack it or have forgotten that I already have it. As Ātman I lack nothing. When I forget I'm the Ātman (think māyā), my ignorance conjures up all sorts of things which I seem to lack, especially things without which life seems unbearable—hence the presence of desires in my heart.

When I choose to use the power of discernment, my primary focus should be on the desirer, not on desire or on the process of desiring. Who is the desirer? Obviously, it is neither the body nor the mind: both are material and both are devoid of consciousness. I am not the desirer either, for I am the Ātman: I lack nothing and I need nothing. But something bizarre seems to have happened (think māyā again). I forgot who I am and the forgetful me has now become the desirer. No longer free and infinite but asleep and dreaming, I see myself as a human being in a world filled with innumerable other beings, all of whom are fighting for survival and hankering after a piece of the pie.

Discernment can stop me from mindlessly joining the rat race. It can help me see things as they really are— and it can help me see *me* as I really am. The more I remind myself of my true nature, the less identified I become with my body and mind. The more power I bring to focus on the real, the more does the dream begin to fade. The more I realize my fullness, the less do

I desire anything. The more I remember I am the Ātman, the less of a desirer I become. Eliminating the desirer from the equation automatically derails the desiring process.

It may not always be easy to dislodge the desirer from the heart. It feels as if the desirer has been around for a long time. Try evicting a stubborn tenant who has lived in an apartment for many years—and you know how difficult it is! Evicting the desirer is infinitely more challenging than that. It is easier to apply discernment to the object of desire before applying it to the desirer.

When viewed from the perspective of the Ātman, desire is irrational. Its presence is quite understandable, though, when seen the through the lens of a finite being with an acute sense of incompleteness. This sense seems so inbuilt, so hardened, that it feels as if we are biologically doomed to always want something or the other. Getting rid of desire feels like an impossible task. The next best thing to do, then, is to focus on *what* is being desired.

Desires can be good or bad. To a spiritual seeker, a good desire is one which leads to the spiritual goal and a bad desire is one which detracts from that goal. Through discernment, I can take a long, hard look at my desires, determine which are "good" and which are "bad," keep the good ones and let go of the bad ones.

How do I determine which desires are good and which are bad? A simple test would be to ask the question: will this make me stronger physically, mentally, intellectually, spiritually—in one or more or all of these ways? If yes, the desire is good. If no, it is bad. My good desires lead to good actions, which purify my heart and make me stronger. In course of time, I become strong enough to apply discernment to my "desirer" identity and am able to shed it with relative ease. Once that happens, it automatically eliminates even the good desires from my heart. This doesn't mean I will stop being or doing good. It simply means I will do good spontaneously and effortlessly, because it has become my second nature, not because I *desire* to do so.

DISCERNMENT AND KARMA

Like the triad of desire, the desirer, and the object of desire, there is the triad of work, the worker, and the object of work. Similar to what was done with desire, discernment is focused not on work or the object of work but on the worker. The question is: *who* is doing the work?

The answer might seem obvious but it is not. Enter discernment. We see at once that every work is done with the help of either body or mind or both. They are as much products of matter as are tables and chairs. The body and the mind have no consciousness of their own. They are only instruments. They are not "doing" any work consciously. That leaves only the Ātman as the possible doer. But the Ātman is consciousness itself, beyond any wants. The Ātman has no need to work since it is free from desire.

It is the *combination* of the Ātman with body/mind which produces the I-sense, creates the need for work, and has the instruments to fulfill that need. Never mind that the Ātman and body/mind don't really combine. We have already seen that their combination is as real as the combination of the rope with a "snake" in a dimly lit room. Nevertheless it *feels* real, due to the machinations of māyā.

Discernment makes us take a closer look at the combination of body/mind and the Ātman. It helps us to separate matter from consciousness. A discerning mind asks: What is work other than objects in the material world interacting with one another following the laws of matter?[42] You are now reading this book. Let's see what is happening here. Made of paper (or some other material if you are reading the digital version), the book is clearly a material object. You are likely holding it in your hand, which is another entity made up entirely of material particles, and reading it with the help of your eyes, another material organ of your body. We can run through the entire mechanism of perception and comprehension, which will include among other things the optic nerve, the brain centers, the mind, and the intellect. All of these things are products of matter.

On their own, none of these things can do anything unless they are powered by consciousness. It is the Ātman which powers the whole enterprise. Consciousness percolates through body and mind, making it appear as if *they* are conscious entities. The

Ātman not only powers the process of holding the book, reading it, and understanding it but also appropriates it as its own. In other words, the māyā-controlled Ātman feels, "I am doing this." If asked, you will likely say, "I am reading the book." Having identified with the body/mind as me (and sometimes as "mine"), the Ātman has transformed itself into the "I" in the statement, "I am reading the book."

With the help of discernment we can disengage the Ātman from both body and mind. It is not necessary for the activity itself to cease on account of that. The activity can—and usually does—go on, but the Ātman does not see itself as "doing" anything. The Ātman remains a detached witness. Imagine the sun to be a detached witness to everything that happens in its light. The sun itself remains unaffected and is not dependent on anyone for its light. The sun continues to shine whether or not there is anyone who needs its light. The Ātman is the sun of consciousness perennially shining whether or not there is anything to be conscious of. That is who I am—consciousness itself.

Like the desirer-me, the worker-me is not easy to dislodge. The sense of being a doer is generally too strong and my power of discernment may lack the force to unmask the doer-me who does all the work. In such cases, it is helpful to first apply discernment to work before it is applied to my identity as the worker. I can focus on the nature of my work and separate good work from bad work.

Several factors play a role in determining whether a work is good or bad. One is the nature of the work itself: any work that is unethical or contrary to the spirit of the scriptures cannot be good. Another factor is the effect on the person who is working: any work that leads to weakness of any kind cannot be good. The third and final factor is how the work impacts others: if it produces more sorrow and suffering, it cannot be good.

A jñāna yogī makes concerted effort to do good work and avoid bad work. Done with patience and perseverance, this practice gradually produces enormous moral strength, which then makes the jñāna yogī capable of disengaging from the "worker" identity and being a detached but alert witness to all the work that is being done by body and mind. Once the Ātman stops seeing itself as the "doer," the link connecting desire and action is dealt another fatal blow.

We have examined the fundamentals of knowledge and ignorance and how the two interact with each other. We have also reviewed the Vedanta framework and seen how the self, the world, and God relate to one another. Discernment is the key practice in jñāna yoga. The karma chain is snapped by looking deeply at both desire and karma, and discovering that I am neither the one who desires nor the one who works. As we have seen, it is all about asking the right questions, examining whatever is before the physical eye or the mind's eye in as unbiased a way as possible. Once the examination yields its results, it's time to make the right choice and to pick the right option.

Ignorance is the root problem and knowledge is the ultimate solution. Only knowledge—and nothing else—can root out ignorance. Wisdom lies in choosing everything that leads to knowledge and letting go of everything that keeps us mired in ignorance. The journey from ignorance to knowledge is powered by discernment. Now we can turn to the nuts and bolts of the discernment practice.

PRACTICE

What is the use of a set of logically organized concepts if they don't eventually lead to tangible results? Results come through practice. The theoretical framework which powers the practice has been mapped out in the preceding chapters. In this chapter we will focus on practice.

Not everyone feels the urge to practice. Even among those who do, not everyone is fit to begin practice. Without adequate fitness, no practice can yield the desired results. How will I know if I am fit (*adhikārī*) for the practice of jñāna yoga? What is required of me to be a jñāna yogī?

Not surprisingly, the first requirement is an interest in jñāna yoga. If jñāna yoga fires up your imagination, if it resonates with your head and heart, then it is the path for you. It is obvious that I am attracted to jñāna yoga. Why else would I have written this book? Since you have picked up this book and have persevered up to this point, chances are you too have more than a casual interest in the subject.

Interest, though, is never enough if not backed up by aptitude. Since discernment is the principal practice in jñāna yoga, we must make sure that we have the skill to practice discernment in a sustained manner. We have already noted the discernment essentials: healthy skepticism, careful examination, and fearless questioning. Add concentration and clarity of mind to the mix, and we are ready for a discernment adventure.[1]

It's an adventure that can yield the highest reward— absolute freedom from every kind of limitation. How hungry we are for this kind of freedom will determine how relentless and unflagging our efforts are. If we long for spiritual freedom as desperately as a drowning person longs for air, we are well on our way to the highest knowledge. The more our longing for knowledge, the more intense will be our efforts and the quicker will be our progress.[2]

These three, then—interest, aptitude and longing—are the requirements to begin the practice. It just so happens that these three basic requirements are related to the three basic practices of jñāna yoga: to hear, to reflect, and to meditate.[3] An interest in jñāna yoga prompts us to "hear" what these texts say. It is our aptitude that equips us to "reflect" on what we have heard, and it is longing that powers our effort to "meditate."

HEAR, REFLECT, MEDITATE

It is interest in a subject that pushes us to make conscious effort to hear about it. What's so special about "hearing" (*śravaṇa*)? To speak of Vedanta as old is an understatement. Vedanta's history goes back to the period when nothing was written: all teaching was oral. The only way to learn anything in those very ancient times was to hear about it from a knowledgeable person. Traditionally, therefore, the preliminary Vedanta practice came to be known as "hearing."

But there is a deeper reason as well. Today we can learn through reading—both on paper as well as on screens of our desktops and mobile devices. Hearing is not outdated, of course, for much of our learning still occurs through listening to lectures and classes, podcasts and audiobooks—not to forget the often unconscious learning that occurs through what we see, taste, touch and smell.

No matter which amongst our senses opens the door to learning, the incoming information needs to be processed by the mind. When we read a text, the mind needs to enter the heart of the text, so to speak, to understand what the message is. Understanding the context and reading between the lines is essential to know what exactly the text is saying. The process of squeezing knowledge out of information is technically known as "hearing."

What does a jñāna yogī "hear" through any and every avenue of learning? In a nutshell, this: Change is the name of the game.[4] Nothing lasts for ever, except the one who perceives the change. No one can ever know or confirm whether the world and everything that we see is real. There may be uncertainty about the object of knowledge, but there is no uncertainty whatsoever about the one who is seeking knowledge: the knower *is* real. I am the knower and my own existence is never in doubt. I know myself but not so well. My understanding of myself seems clouded. When I know who I *really* am—in other words, when the knower is known—all my doubts vanish: freedom, bliss and immortality replace bondage, suffering and mortality.

As we have seen, the basic problem is ignorance—and only knowledge can remove ignorance. If I am ignorant of the truth, I only have to "hear" the truth from someone who knows it. I have forgotten that I am the Ātman and all I need is someone to remind me of who I really am. That should solve the problem—and it indeed does for an extraordinarily gifted (*uttama*) student who is ready in every way. That's all the "practice" such a student needs: just hearing the truth.

But most of us are not ready yet. We hear the truth: it makes sense to us intellectually, but it doesn't make us enlightened spiritually. Our ignorance doesn't quit. It stubbornly stands its ground with a host of questions and doubts (*asambhāvanā*). No matter how often I am told that I am the immortal, pure and perfect Ātman, it just seems too much of a fancy. How can I be one with the whole universe? How can I even consider the possibility of oneness in the face of such stupendous diversity which won't just disappear? How can this world that I see not be out there really? When such questions fill the heart, the second practice becomes essential: I must reflect (*manana*) on what I have heard.

Reflecting gives me a chance to take a hard second look at the doubts in my mind and understand how both unity and diversity are possible, one really real and the other only apparently so. Ignorance has the extraordinary ability to make the impossible seem possible. What we perceive and how we perceive it depends on the ability of the senses and the tendencies in the mind. What doesn't depend on the senses and the mind is the perceiver, who remains unchanged. Such are the kind of insights produced through reflection. When doubts are put to rest, knowledge usually dawns in the hearts of moderately gifted (*madhyama*) students, freeing them from ignorance. But even the practice of reflection may not be enough for everyone.

The humbling truth is that most of us belong to the lowest (*kaniṣṭha*) category of jñāna yogīs. We are beset with not only doubts but also a more serious obstacle: contrary thoughts (*viparīta-bhāvanā*). In spite of my hearing and reflection, what if I still cannot shake off the feeling that I am a mortal, weak, ignorant human being? What if I continue to feel that my body/mind *are* real, the world *is* real, and I *am* different from the supreme being? If such is my present conviction, I need not only to hear the truth and reflect on it but also to continue my struggle with the third practice: I should meditate (*nididhyāsana*).

Meditation is a deeper form of inner exploration and it must be practiced until the last major obstacle— contrary thoughts—falls by the wayside and knowledge results. Meditation in jñāna yoga involves intense effort to prevent one's identification with body/mind and to maintain the awareness of the Ātman to the exclusion of everything else.[5] When this is achieved effortlessly, meditation is transformed into total absorption (*samādhi*). If I pull a branch of a tree and bend it down with effort, it reverts to its original position when I let it go. But if a branch of the tree bends down on its own, without any external effort, it remains bent. Similar is the difference between meditation and absorption. When there is effort involved, it is meditation. When the practice becomes completely effortless, it is absorption.[6]

The practice of jñāna yoga begins with "hearing" and— except when enlightenment occurs immediately after hearing—is generally followed by reflection and meditation. Once begun, these don't really appear as three distinct practices to be employed in a chronological order. They somehow merge and become a unified practice, through which hearing keeps getting clearer, reflection keeps removing doubts, and meditation keeps clearing the fog of misperception. The three practices are interlinked: they reinforce one

another and evolve together. The reason the three
practices go hand in hand is that they all involve the
mind, primarily the mind's capacity to think. Jñāna yoga
is impossible without the ability to think clearly and
wisely.

THINKING

The power of thought is the most underrated power in
the world.[7] Thoughts are subtle, invisible and belong to
the inner world: no one apart from ourselves knows
what's going on in our heads. Actions are gross, visible
and belong to the external world: others see what we do
unless we prevent them from doing so. As a result, we
are judged more by what we *do* or *don't* do than by what
we *think*. This encourages us to be more mindful of our
actions than of our thoughts. And that's a problem.

What defines our identity and shapes our personality is
not so much what we *do* but what we *think*—and *how* we
think. Thoughts are the source from which words and
actions emerge.[8] In an integrated personality, both
words and actions are visible expressions of the thinking
process. Who is an authentic person? One whose
thoughts, words and actions are in perfect sync.

But such perfectly integrated individuals are rare. Most of
us muddle through life blissfully unaware of even the need
for integration. What we think is unconnected with what
we say. What we say is unconnected with what we do.
What we say and do at present is likely to be unconnected

with what we say and do only a few hours later. An aspiring jñāna yogī cannot afford to live that way. A life consciously focused on harmonizing one's thoughts, words and actions is high on the list of a jñāna yogī's practice.

It all begins with right thinking. Especially, thinking rightly about oneself—specifically, about one's *self*.[9] As we have seen, the subject and the object are dynamically related. How I perceive the world depends on how I perceive myself.[10] We often make the mistake of trying to change our perception without changing the perceiver. The reason I have no difficulty seeing others as human beings is that I have no difficulty seeing myself as a human being. But I struggle and fail to see everyone as a child of God because I struggle and fail to see *myself* as a child of God. If I wish to see the presence of God everywhere, I must begin by seeing the presence of God within me. Every change in my "me" brings about a corresponding change in how this "me" experiences everything else.

A primary jñāna yoga practice is to examine where my "me" is located and make sure that it is in the right place. It is significant that the Sanskrit term for a healthy person is *svastha*, literally, "one who dwells in the Ātman" (*sva*=self, Ātman; *stha*=to dwell).[11] The term for a sick person is *asvastha*, "one who does *not* dwell in the Ātman." I may be physically and mentally healthy, but when I see myself as body/mind ("I am a human being," "I am worried"), I am nevertheless spiritually sick. When I see myself as the Ātman ("I am birthless

and deathless," "I am pure and perfect"), I am
spiritually healthy.

I feel contented and fulfilled when I see myself as I truly
am. I suffer when I see myself as someone else—when I
see myself as a human being, for instance. Whenever my
"I" locates itself in the Ātman, I feel free and immortal,
pure and perfect. When my "I" becomes submerged in
the sinking sands of humanness, I tether myself to all
the imperfections of body and mind. I become mortal,
afflicted with illness, anxious about aging, and stressed
with problems aplenty.

Seeing myself as a spirit does not mean that I deny or
become blind to my human identity. It's just that my
humanness remains somehow less real, almost like a
faded backdrop to my true identity as the Ātman. I am
not a human being trying to become the Ātman. I am
the Ātman playing the role of a human being.
Shakespeare was on to something when he wrote, "All
the world's a stage." Had he been around today, he
might have been tempted to write: "All the world's a 3D
movie."

It sure is—a 3D movie which we can view for free.
Rather than enjoy this free movie, it's astounding that
people choose to pay in order to see movies which are
not even half as interesting. Why subscribe to Netflix
when I have a free membership to Worldflix! I'm not
able to enjoy this free movie of the world because,
instead of being a viewer, I have become an actor. I have
become so good an actor that I have lost myself in my

role and forgotten my true identity. I no longer remember that I am the Ātman. I am now fully immersed in my role as a human being.

As long as I enjoy being in character, I don't need to change anything. But a time will come when it is no longer fun. Worse, it may get positively torturous or, at the very least, boring. When that happens, I need not despair. I have the option to call it a day. I have the option to wash off the makeup and get back to being myself.[12] I can then choose to sit and watch the cosmic 3D movie for a while and enjoy it in the way I never could have enjoyed it as an actor.[13] Or I can choose to walk out and be free for ever. The spiritually illumined amongst us are those who have achieved the freedom to watch the cosmic movie until they decide enough is enough.

When the body/mind costume is shed, the Ātman alone abides in all its divine glory. Caution: both body *and* mind need to go for ever. When only the body goes, that is death, not enlightenment. The mind survives and returns with a new body and the torture continues until I am able to locate myself permanently in the Ātman.

A jñāna yogī makes a conscious effort to locate the "I" in the Ātman. No matter how often this is forgotten, no matter how often the "I" gravitates towards the body and mind, the jñāna yogī drags it back to the Ātman with patience and perseverance. It's not easy because the mind has become recalcitrant. Old habits die hard.

TAMING OF THE MIND

Granted it is not easy to teach an old dog new tricks, but nothing is impossible. No matter how old a dog is, there is at least a little bit of the puppy present in every dog's heart. With age the body becomes feeble, but a part of the dog's mind is always in puppy mode, enthusiastic as ever. If we can connect with that puppy, the dog will learn new things easily. Our mind is considerably older than the body. The same mind has been with us through all of our past lives, whereas the body has been around only since this birth. Training the mind is not easy, but it is possible if we can reach the "puppy" within it.

The "puppy" within the mind is sometimes called the "higher" mind. It is always alert and filled with inexhaustible energy. The rest of the mind is the "lower" mind, the part that is tired, bored, unimaginative, and stuck in a rut. The mind is one but it is divided, sort of. Which is how we are able to speak about a higher mind and a lower mind. The terminology in different disciplines may vary and the divisions may be conceived in different ways. The well known divisions in psychology are the conscious mind and the unconscious mind. In mysticism we also hear about another segment called the superconscious mind. It is enough for our purpose to recognize that the mind is not monolithic: it is more dynamic than the body, more subtle, more powerful, and a lot more complex.

A small part of our mind seems to absorb (and hence reflect) consciousness more than the rest of the mind does. What this means is that through this small part—which I call the "higher mind"—it is easier for me to locate myself in the Ātman. It is in the higher mind that the power of spiritual intuition is activated.[14] Compared to this higher mind, the rest of the mind is "lower." The higher mind is still a "layer," but a significantly more transparent layer than the lower mind, which can range from being translucent to almost opaque. My efforts need to be focused on using the higher mind to raise the lower mind. The higher mind is already my friend, the lower mind sometimes acts like an enemy.[15] The goal is to make the entire mind my friend and fill it with the light of consciousness.

What the lower mind lacks is determination, discipline and clarity. The jñāna yoga practice, therefore, is structured around developing these qualities. Determination is developed through introspection: when we keep reminding ourselves about the fragility of life and the uncertainty about the future, our resolve to get out of the karma-tangle is strengthened.[16] We become more determined to pursue the goal. This leads to a more rigorous practice of discernment at all times. Discernment shines through every thought, every word, and every action of a jñāna yogī.

Discipline is developed through sticking to a self-evolved course of practice which is powered by determination to succeed. A jñāna yogī develops a "routine" of thoughts to think and things to do—and sticks to that routine come what may. The mind is a creature of habit. A disciplined routine makes the practice of discernment easy and relatively effortless.

Clarity is developed through purity of life, with conscious practice of thinking positive thoughts, cultivating healthy relationships, and doing only what is right and good.[17] In other words, doing all work in the spirit of karma yoga and not straying from the path of dharma make the mind pure and the perceptions clear. The more the clarity, the better is the practice of discernment.

One of the practices that helps develop all three—determination, discipline and clarity—is worship. This may sound odd, as "worship" is normally associated with the yoga of devotion. This is really unfortunate, since worship—depending on how it's done—is useful in all the four yogas of Swami Vivekananda. In a Vedantic form of worship the divine within is ritually externalized and, after offerings are made, the divine is withdrawn back into the heart. The worship is then concluded after seeking forgiveness for ascribing form to what lies beyond form and for objectifying what really is always the subject. A daily worship, done with faith and steadfastness, is a great help to a jñāna yogī.

With increasing determination, discipline and clarity it becomes easier to tame the rebellious part of the mind and make the *entire* mind our friend whose judgment we can totally rely on. With the blessings of such a mind, the practice of jñāna yoga is a breeze.

JÑĀNA YOGA PRACTICE

How does a jñāna yogī's day begin? Typically, with Ātman-remembrance (ātma-smṛti). As the day progresses, the jñāna yogī finds creative ways to stay connected with the Ātman (yuktātmā). When it's time to retire for the night, the jñāna yogī rests in the light of the Ātman, like a baby resting in her mother's lap: "I take refuge in the light of the Ātman (ātmadīpa), which shines even where there is no mother, no father, no friend, no brother, no beloved, and no knowledge of day or night."[18] The jñāna yoga practice revolves around the light of the Ātman—and it keeps at it until the light totally engulfs the jñāna yogī, dissolving all material coverings, leaving only the Ātman shining with pristine purity.[19]

There are several concrete ways through which remembrance, connectedness, and taking refuge can be practiced. Here are a few possibilities.

MORNING

Soon after waking up, even before I get out of bed, the first thing I need to do is to remind myself of my spiritual identity. Repeating even a part of an affirmation such as the following can be helpful:

I am detached, independent and imperishable. My nature is pure existence, consciousness and bliss. I am ever free from the three sorrows and distinct from the three states. The light of consciousness is inside me and outside me—it is my own light, for I am the blessed One.[20]

Another well-known composition is Śaṅkarācārya's *Nirvāṇa-Ṣatkam* ("Six Verses on Nirvāṇa"), which can serve the same purpose.[21] There is a special class of compositions for morning remembrance (*prātaḥ-smaraṇa-stotra*). Here is one which can be useful to a jñāna yogī:

It's morning—the time to remember that I am the Ātman, the existence-consciousness-bliss absolute, the transcendent Supreme Being shining in the heart. I am not a material object. I am Brahman, the goal of the highest spiritual seekers, the indivisible and eternal witness of the three states—dream, waking and deep sleep.

It's morning—the time to meditate on the eternal, imperishable God of gods, who is beyond the reach of thoughts and words, whose grace makes all senses shine, and who is described by the Vedas as "not this, not this."

It's morning—the time to bow down to the eternal, infinite, and effulgent Supreme Being, who is beyond the darkness of ignorance, on whom this entire world is projected like a snake on a rope.[22]

If the morning begins on a positive note, it sets the direction for the rest of the day. The morning hours are precious and they shouldn't be wasted. Lose an hour in the morning, as they say, and you will be searching for it the rest of the day. The practice of remembering and affirming one's spiritual identity is reinforced through prayer, japa and meditation. Receiving instructions from a teacher (*guru*) enhances the power and quality of these practices.

THROUGHOUT THE DAY

Beginning the day with self-remembrance is not really difficult. With a little bit of determination, the practice becomes natural and effortless. What is difficult is to *maintain* that awareness throughout the day. As we delve into the daily round of duties and responsibilities, it is easy to forget what was affirmed in the morning. It is easy to forget that I am the divine, immortal Ātman— and resume behaving as if I am simply this body and mind, merely human and mortal.

The best way to maintain spiritual awareness is to find creative ways to remind ourselves of things that we tend to forget. Can we find opportunities to remain connected with our true nature even as we engage in seemingly mundane daily chores? Chanting of prayers or hymns at fixed hours has been found helpful. Many try to repeat their mantra now and then, even if the repetition is limited to barely a minute or less. Another

way is to practice self-remembrance before beginning
every new activity.

Taking help of scriptural passages and prayers is good,
but we are also free to compose our own reminders that
best express our practice and ideal. Before I begin to
clean my room, for instance, I can say something like
this to myself:

> *My own room*
> *Is an extension of my mind.*
> *When I clean my room,*
> *My mind becomes clear.*

Here are a few more samples. Before picking up the
phone or joining a conversation:

> *Words are powerful*
> *And time is precious.*
> *I'll listen with attention*
> *And speak with a clear mind.*

Before a meal:

> *Food preserves life.*
> *Wasting food is wasting life.*
> *I'll eat slowly, responsibly,*
> *And with gratitude.*

Before beginning work:

My body and mind are instruments.
I'll care for them and use them well.
When they are nourished,
I feel strong and happy.

While getting into a car:

A car travels fast,
The mind travels faster.
Let me use them both
With care and caution.

Before meeting people:

Every person I meet,
Is, like me, the Ātman.
May I always treat others
With love and respect.

Simple as these words are, such brief affirmations—
when done with sincerity and regularity—are
surprisingly powerful: they help maintain awareness and
prevent us from getting sucked back into the
unconscious stream of worldly life.

Another way to maintain awareness is to practice
mindful breathing. Every now and then, or whenever we
remember to do so, it is helpful to take a deep breath
consciously while silently reminding oneself, "I am the
Ātman," and then breathe out slowly as we look around,
saying mentally, "Everything is filled with divine

presence." Over time, this kind of practice becomes natural and there is less forgetfulness.

The forms and sounds in the world may be fleeting, but behind and beyond all the changes stands the unchanging reality, the divine which seemingly manifests as the world.[23] The perceiver is the divine manifesting as the ego. That which is perceived is the divine manifesting as the world. The subject/object divide eventually disappears in undifferentiated (*nirvikalpa*) samādhi—and the divine alone remains.

The best time to begin the practice is immediately after waking up: I can try to take a peaceful, deep breath while still in bed, and say to myself: "I am the Ātman," and then breathe out calmly and fully while saying, "All this is Brahman" or "Everything is filled with divine presence." As I slowly get out of bed, I can make a resolve to maintain that awareness throughout the day. No matter how often I forget it, every time I breathe in and out mindfully, it will be easy to bring myself back to my Ātman identity.

Periodic self-questioning also helps. Whenever I am not sure about the appropriateness of my words or actions, I can ask myself: "Is this how the Ātman will speak? Is this how the Ātman will work? Is this how the Ātman will think?" Of course, we know that the Ātman's "speaking," "working" and "thinking" occur through the body and mind, but such questioning is a way to affirm that both body and mind are only instruments under the control of the Ātman, not vice versa.

BEFORE RETIRING

It is helpful to quickly review the day's major events before sleeping, as that gives us a good idea of where we did well and where we messed up. With a firm resolve to not repeat the day's mistakes, the jñāna yogī surrenders once again to the inner light: "I take refuge in the light of the Ātman (*ātmadīpa*), which shines even where there is no mother, no father, no friend, no brother, no beloved, and no knowledge of day or night." Come morning, it's time to begin the day again with self-remembrance and a firm resolve to maintain that awareness.

If I want to be a jñāna yogī, I am expected to maintain such awareness throughout the day until I fall asleep and throughout my life until I die.[24] There is no vacation from the practice of jñāna yoga until I know who I really am. When the knower is known, the vacation begins and it doesn't ever end. I never have to go back to "work" again.

PERIODICALLY

Just as physical exercises keep the body healthy, spiritual exercises keep the spirit healthy—meaning, they help me remain rooted in the Ātman, my true self, not buried under the layers of the body and the mind. Besides the exercises done daily, a few can be done periodically, at least once a week or a fortnight or a month, depending on one's schedule and level of interest.

The most important among these periodic exercises is a
deep exploration of one's self. The process is simple
enough: to look really hard and really deep at who I am.
This can be done in at least three ways: by examining (1)
the levels of subject-object relationships around me, (2)
the states of waking, dream and deep sleep, and (3) the
layers of body, mind and ego. For this practice, I can
either meditate on a scriptural passage or simply apply
reason—in either case, my ultimate goal should be to
confirm the results through direct experience.

What I know of the world comes through the sensations
of sight, sound, smell, touch, and taste. The senses are
my windows to the world. My eyes, for instance, see the
world: my eyes are the "seer" and the world is the "seen."
The sensory data that the eyes bring is presented to the
mind. The mind then becomes the "seer" and the eyes—
along with the information they gather—are transformed
into the "seen." After the information is cataloged by the
mind, it is passed on to the intellect, which then assumes
the role of the "seer" and the mind becomes the "seen."
Finally the Ātman—the conscious witness—makes the
whole process come alive and becomes the "seer,"
transforming the intellect into the "seen."

Every "seer" in this integrated process—the senses, the
mind, the intellect—is provisional except the Ātman, the
real me, who is the true "seer." Everything other than me
is an object of my perception. I am the eternal,
unchanging subject.[25] I am the "knower," everything
else is the object of my knowledge. This is the way

discernment is practiced with regard to subject-object relationships.

How should I practice discernment with regard to the three states of waking, dream, deep sleep? When awake I see the world while dwelling inside my body. When asleep I see the dream-world while dwelling inside my dream-body. In deep sleep I see nothing and I am not aware of my body—but I'm still present. How else do I remember later my experience of both a kind of nothingness and a kind of bliss in deep sleep? What is experienced in the three states changes, but the experiencer remains the same.

My apparent identity and the contents of my experience —in other words, what I am conscious of—seem to change in the three states. The *objects* of my consciousness keep changing but the *subject*, the perceiver, who is consciousness itself, remains the same. The constant and unchanging consciousness—the "knower"— is who I am. Everything other than me is an ever changing froth of names and forms.[26]

To practice discernment with regard to the layers over the Ātman, I can look at my body and see that over the years it has changed, slowly but surely. When I put an old picture of mine next to a recent one, the change looks quite drastic. I then look at my mind and similarly find great changes: my way of thinking, my hopes, concerns, interests and feelings have changed— "evolved," as some might say. The same is true with regard to the functioning of my intellect and my sense of who I am.

And yet, notwithstanding all these obvious changes that have occurred with the passage of time, I still think of myself as the same person. Something has remained unchanged. There is something in my "me" which holds all the changing pieces together and provides them with a sense of unity. That unchanging core of my being is the *real* me. My body, mind, intellect, ego—all of these are coverings, which often pretend to be me. But when I look deeply at myself—at my "self"—I know that I am different from them all. They change, I don't. They are perishable, I am not.[27]

This is the general direction in which the inner exploration may proceed, no matter whether I am thinking about the subject-object relationships, the three states of waking, dream and deep sleep, or the different layers of my personality. The practice doesn't have to follow the same pattern always. In fact, it shouldn't. All that I need is to find time and a quiet place to withdraw my mind from everything outside and point it inward, keeping the light of awareness shining and the power of discernment guiding the search. Let the exploration take its own course. This is not a ritual. This should not also become a chore that needs to be hurried through. The inner exploration is a conscious, deliberate practice done with the help of a focused and determined mind.

The inner exploration often leads to a meditative state and visualization is a great help in such exercises. Sri

Ramakrishna's teacher Tota Puri offered the following image when he instructed his disciple:

[The supreme being] is like an infinite ocean—water everywhere, to the right, left, above, and below. Water enveloped in water. It is the water of the Great Cause, motionless. Waves spring up when it becomes active. Its activities are creation, preservation and destruction.[28]

Swami Vivekananda once taught the following meditation, which can be used by any of us:

Above, it is full of me; below, it is full of me; in the middle, it is full of me. I am in all beings, and all beings are in me. *Om Tat Sat*, I am It. I am existence above mind. I am the one spirit of the universe. I am neither pleasure nor pain. The body drinks, eats, and so on. I am not the body. I am not mind. I am He. I am the witness. I look on. When health comes I am the witness. When disease comes I am the witness. I am Existence, Knowledge, Bliss. I am the essence and nectar of knowledge. Through eternity I change not. I am calm, resplendent, and unchanging.[29]

Another helpful practice for a budding jñāna yogī is to make an effort to look at everything subjectively.[30] Our general tendency is to look at things and ask why they are the way they are. That may spur us to go change whatever is wrong in the world which, in itself, is not a bad thing. Except that such attempts seldom succeed in bringing about a lasting change, the world being what it is and what it has always been.[31] A jñāna yogī takes a more pragmatic view and asks, "Why am I seeing those things in this way?" What is perceived outside, after all, is not totally independent of my own perception. So it makes sense to question my perception before questioning what is perceived. If I change the way I see things, the things I see change miraculously for me.

It is likely that, in the beginning at least, I may not be able to maintain the intensity of all of these practices for long. That is quite all right. There is no need to force myself too hard. But done with regularity and faith, these practices gather strength and momentum over time and become powerful. An underlying awareness of my true self begins to grow and persist longer than it did before. With a newly discovered self-identity, the world begins to look different. A new "me" sees a new "world" —a world covered by the light of the divine.[32]

The truth, however, is that it is not the light of the divine that covers the world. On the contrary, it was the world all along that was covering the light of the divine. The cumulative practices of hearing, reflection, and meditation *un*-cover the light of the divine when the ever-changing bubbles of names and forms burst for ever. The world was never as real as it seemed. My identity as a human being and my perception of the world were as false as the "snake" I saw in place of a rope in my semi-lit room.

What is never false is the one who is experiencing all this. The experiencer, or the knower, is real. The knower is unfettered by the limits of time, space and causality. That which is never bound in any way is infinite and eternal. If it's infinite, it's one. Not two, not many. Just one.

ONENESS

*T*hroughout this book, two words appear often: "consciousness" and "knowledge." While these words are obviously related, they also convey ideas that seem fairly distinct. Consciousness is generally viewed as a precondition for knowledge. If I am not conscious of the world—such as when I am asleep—I have no knowledge of the world. Consciousness, therefore, necessarily has to precede knowledge. I *first* become conscious of a thing's presence and *then* I know what it is.

Let's say I open my eyes and see a tree. This might seem to be instantaneous, but there are actually two events that occur one after another with lightning speed: (1) I open my eyes and become conscious of an object, and (2) I know that the object is a tree. Of these, #1 is generic (*sāmānya*) knowledge and #2 is specific (*viśeṣa*) knowledge. Generic knowledge, at its most generic level, is simply the knowledge of existence. Consciousness gives us generic knowledge. The instant we are conscious of something, we know that it exists, either out in the world or in our minds. If it exists, we may be able to know more about it. If a thing doesn't exist, the question of knowing it doesn't arise.

The generic knowledge is always valid but the specific knowledge doesn't have to be. It could be erroneous, such as when I enter a semi-lit room, become *conscious* of an object lying on the ground ("generic knowledge") and then *know* it to be a snake ("specific knowledge"), an error that is discovered only when a closer look reveals a rope where the "snake" was. Something similar has happened to every one of us on a very personal level as well. My generic knowledge of myself is that I exist, and that's absolutely true. My specific knowledge of myself is that I am a mortal human being: this is an error. Produced by my ignorance, the error can only be removed by acquiring the knowledge of who I *really* am.

In English, the word "consciousness" is usually related to generic knowledge (the knowledge of "is-ness") whereas the word "knowledge" is used to denote the specifics of who, what, when and how. Sanskrit does have words like *cit* and *caitanya,* which denote "consciousness," and *vidyā,* which denotes "knowledge." But the word, *jñāna,* is special: it manages to convey the ideas associated with both "consciousness" and "knowledge." *Jñāna* can denote both generic knowledge as well as specific knowledge, and is used in both those senses in Sanskrit texts.[1]

SELF-KNOWLEDGE

Śaunaka's question—posed at the beginning of this
book—uses a derivative of the word *jñāna*: "What is it
knowing which everything becomes known?"[2] Since
jñāna can denote "consciousness" as well, the question
can also be translated thus: "What is it being conscious
of which we become conscious of everything?" In
retrospect, the answer seems fairly commonsensical:
"Get to know the primary source of consciousness and
you'll be conscious of everything." The source of
consciousness is my own real self, the Ātman.
Consciousness is the very nature of the Ātman.[3]

Since the Ātman is my own self, being conscious of the
Ātman is different from being conscious of an object
like, say, a table. My consciousness of a table produces
the knowledge: "*This* is a table." My consciousness of
the Ātman produces the knowledge: "*I* am the Ātman."
I don't so much have to say this as to *experience* it. At
present I don't need to say, "I am a human being," I just
know it: it's an integral part of my experience. In the
same way, a time will come when I'll know that I am the
Ātman: it will becomes an integral part of my
experience. Abiding for ever in that experience is what
self-realization or self-knowledge (*ātma-jñāna*) means.

When I experience the Ātman, I'll no longer have any
doubts and I'll know everything.[4] "Everything?"—I
asked an elderly monk years ago. His answer was: "No,
not quite. If you didn't know how to fly a plane before
your spiritual illumination, you won't be able to fly a

plane simply because you know you are the Ātman."[5]
He explained to me that a self-realized person no longer
has any doubt regarding the only thing that is really real,
the Ātman. Everything else is only an appearance. The
things we perceive (this includes my own body and
mind) are nothing more than a shimmering dance of
fragile forms, sounds and ideas[6]—and the perception of
even these is preceded by the consciousness of their
apparent presence, which becomes possible because of
the Ātman. In reality the Ātman alone exists, and that is
why knowing (or becoming conscious of) the Ātman is
the same as knowing "everything."[7]

In other words, *not* knowing the Ātman I really know
nothing of abiding value. The knowledge of the
perishable things of this world is also perishable. It keeps
me tied to the never-ending circular journey of repeated
births and deaths. Over and over and over again I find
myself embedded in the boringly familiar story which is
enacted on life's stage from birth to death. It's a
perennial drama whose basic script remains unchanged
and no sooner it ends than it begins all over again: death
follows birth which is followed by death, which again …
you get the idea.

Knowing the Ātman gets me out of the crushing circle
by revealing to me that the circle never really existed to
begin with. The circle and everything in it was a
misperception, like seeing a "snake" in place of a rope
in a semi-lit room. The ignorance of the Ātman (rope)
creates the body-mind "me" (snake). The knowledge of
the Ātman destroys the body-mind me. The Ātman

alone remains. It is indestructible and immortal.[8] It is full and complete. It lacks nothing. Most importantly, I no longer see the Ātman as "it." When I know the Ātman, I know that it is the *real* me. I know that I am indestructible and immortal. I alone exist. I am everything. There is nothing apart from me.

THE OCEAN AND ITS WAVES

The ocean is one, its waves are innumerable. The ocean is an enduring presence, but the waves arise and subside. A wave might think of herself as finite and perishable. That would seem to be an accurate view. What if the wave were to begin practicing discernment and take a second, hard look at herself? She might discover that she is made of the same water that comprises the ocean. She is born *from* the ocean, all of her movements are *in* the ocean, and when she dies she returns *to* the ocean. She may begin to wonder whether, apart from a form and a name she carries for some time, she is any different from the ocean. Both are, after all, nothing but the same water. What separates them is perishable; what unites them is perennial. Maybe she and the ocean were never really different to begin with? The reflection of a discerning wave naturally leads to that conclusion—and the wave is right![9]

You and I are waves: we rise and we fall, and we call this birth and death. As long as we remain absorbed in our wave-identity, we'll never discover the ocean that lies all around us.[10] If we open our eyes really wide and look deeply, we'll discover ourselves in the midst of the ocean of material particles. This human body, after all, is only a bunch of atoms and molecules, or protons, neutrons and electrons if we dig deeper. All these particles are held together by a force we call "life" (*prāṇa*). More particles are added to my body through the nourishment provided by food. The body eliminates the unneeded portions of whatever is taken in. My body is a wave in this cosmic ocean, continually exchanging material with it. The body-wave is sustained by the ocean of atoms and molecules. As the wave moves in the ocean, it experiences growth, change, decline and finally death.[11]

Going beyond the ocean of material particles, I encounter a subtle ocean: the ocean of ideas, thoughts and feelings. My mind is a wave in this ocean. My little mind-wave bobs up and down in the cosmic ocean, continually exchanging ideas, thoughts and feelings. My mind may mull over an idea, or be absorbed in some thought, or be overwhelmed with a powerful feeling. I may think of these as "mine"—*my* ideas, *my* thoughts, *my* feelings. But they are no more mine than they are yours. They belong to the ocean of the cosmic mind.[12] They enter into my little wave-mind and I appropriate them as my own. Is any water in the wave really her own? The wave owes her very existence to the ocean. The ocean is continually replenishing the wave-water. The only thing apparently constant about the wave is her wave-identity defined by her name and form.[13]

Explorers shouldn't stop until they reach the end. The story doesn't end with the two oceans—the ocean of material particles and the ocean of thoughts, ideas and feeling. Both of these oceans belong to the perishable, constantly changing material world. Courage is needed to let go of all material supports, physical or mental, and to enter the domain of the spirit, which transcends matter. If I persevere in my effort to look beyond what's obvious, I will discover the ocean of consciousness.[14]

The Ātman identified with my body-mind is a little wave in the infinite ocean of consciousness. Because the Ātman seems to dwell inside a body-mind, I may think of it as the inner self (*pratyagātman*) and distinguish it from the larger, all-pervading, supreme self (*paramātman*). The inner self remains "inner" as long it doesn't shed its body-mind identity and the supreme self is "supreme" only when compared to the self that is trapped inside a body-mind. When the wave subsides, only the ocean remains. When the body-mind identity disappears, the adjectives "inner" and "supreme" become superfluous. The Ātman is all that remains—one and infinite.[15]

If we want to get the language right, we cannot even speak of the Ātman as one and infinite. No one can really express what the Ātman is. Nor is there any need to. The Ātman is who I am, all I need to do is to *experience* it. Nevertheless, it is important to recognize that, if we must speak about the Ātman accurately, we can only say what the Ātman is not. We can say, for instance, that the Ātman has no peer (*a-dvaita*, "non-dual") and the Ātman is *not* finite (*an-anta*, "un-ending"). Every time the Ātman is said to be one and infinite, we must remember the implication.

Because the Ātman is one, it is infinite, and vice versa. The presence of anything else would make the Ātman finite. There *is* nothing else. Not even the physical and mental oceans of gross and subtle matter.[16] They disappear in the same way the "snake" disappears when the rope is seen as a rope. When the ocean of consciousness looms into view, the oceans in which my body and mind dwell fade away. After all, they owed their existence to the ocean of consciousness in the same way the "snake" owed its existence to the rope. When my little Ātman wave attached to a body-mind merges inside the Ātman ocean, the Ātman alone remains.[17] The Ātman is one without a second—and I am that one. This is what I'll experience when I pursue the practices of hearing, reflection and meditation with patience, perseverance and single-minded attention.[18]

THE LOST PRINCE

Vedanta teachers tell the story of a prince, the only heir to a kingdom, who was kidnapped as a baby and remained untraced for nearly two decades. When the king died and his men fanned out to make yet another search for the lost prince, they finally found him deep inside a forest in the home of a hunter couple. The prince's identity was confirmed through a birth mark. The hunter couple confessed to having found the baby abandoned inside the forest. The bewildered young man was escorted back to the palace and preparations were set afoot to install him as the next king.

Although the young man was a prince from the moment he was born, most of his life until that point had been spent thinking of himself as a son of his hunter parents. His life turned topsy-turvy when, out of the blue, the king's men came and told him who he really was. It was a herculean struggle for the prince not only to adjust to the drastic change in his self-identity but also to live, move and talk like a prince, not as a forest-dwelling hunter. He had no idea what a princely life was and what its protocols were.

The prince's story is your and my story. It is the story of every living being. Every one of us is a lost prince. I am the lost Ātman. Long back—no one knows when—I was taken away and abandoned in the forest of the world, which raised me as a human being. I saw myself as a mortal creature for a long time—no one knows how long—until I learned from Vedanta that, in fact, I'm the Ātman. The idea that I am not just human but really divine seems at first to be funny, audacious, even crazy. But slowly it all begins to make sense when I hear about it repeatedly, reflect over it deeply, and meditate on what it really means to be divine.

It doesn't take too long before I realize that I am the Ātman even when I don't know it. I am the Ātman even when I think I am a human being. The twin powers of ignorance—to cover and to project—hide my identity and substitute it with a false identity. As long as I labor under the false identity, I lose all the benefits of my true identity. Thus it is that being the Ātman and not knowing it is as bad as *not* being the Ātman.

But the transition to knowing that I am the Ātman is far from easy. After spending God-knows-how-many lives thinking of myself as a mortal, it is difficult to wake up one fine morning and start seeing myself as immortal. After spending years as a hunter in the forest, it wasn't easy for the young man to see himself as a prince, even though that's who he always was. A jñāna yogī's experience is similar: the struggle, the setbacks, the occasional successes and the more frequent failures—all of these need to be taken in my stride when I begin the practices of hearing, reflection and meditation.

BEFORE THE DAWN

In the beginning my old habit of seeing myself as a human being will try to pull me back every time I try to maintain the awareness of my Ātman identity. Nevertheless, every little success—even if it lasts for only a few seconds, or for a few minutes at the most—will fill the heart with a rare kind of joy. It is relatively easy to do this when alone, but gradually, with some effort, it must be practiced in the company of others as well.

It's good to begin the day with a firm determination to hold on to the thought, "I am the Ātman."[19] Invariably I will forget this after some time. But no sooner I realize I've forgotten it than I must return to being mindful of my Ātman identity. No need for me to feel bad or frustrated by the lapse. I just need to return calmly to being the Ātman, and continue doing my daily chores, maintaining the awareness of being the Ātman.

Will my Ātman identity get in the way of the things I need to do in the course of the day? Absolutely not. It may feel a bit odd for a while, but only for a while. My Ātman identity will recede to the background, or settle in a corner of my heart, always present but never obtrusive. After all, when we have a persistent headache, we are capable of going about our daily chores even when the headache is painful and irritating. It shouldn't be any more difficult to do everything with a persistent Ātman awareness—especially considering that, unlike being a person with a headache, being the Ātman with its inherent joy is most energizing and fulfilling.

Sure, life will not exactly remain same as before. Some of the things that made sense earlier may no longer do so. Other things which I barely noticed or took interest in may appear to be meaningful and interesting. My changing persona and interests may puzzle some friends and irritate others. But at least a few will notice the change in a positive light and will be appreciative. If I lose a few old friends, I'll gain many new ones who share my ideas and ideals.

When I persist with the practices of hearing, reflection and meditation, I'll discover that I'm able to remain mindful and in control of myself longer than I did before. Fewer of my actions will be mechanical. I'll find myself becoming calmer, more peaceful, more contented. The greater the peace I find within me, the more the peace my personality will exude. The greater the love in my heart, the more will I able to love everything and everyone around me.[20]

It won't be only a subjective change. When I change, the world changes for me, it's true, but the change in me also influences the world, at least the world immediately around me. When my heart is filled with peace, those who come in touch with me are able to feel that peace and benefit from it. When my heart is filled with love, it not only eliminates hatred, anger and jealousy from my heart but also makes it easier for others around me to let go of the negativities in their hearts. The service that an enlightened being offers to the world by just being enlightened is seldom recognized because, in spite of its profound power, it is subtle, gentle, and transformative without being invasive.[21]

Life will change when the sun of knowledge rises on the horizon of my heart. The world will look different because I will be different. More accurately, my "I" will be different. It will have cut its cord from the body/mind for ever and it will be what it always was—pure, free and immortal. What this free "I" of mine will see no one but me will know. But what will others see in me?

Many Vedanta texts describe the characteristics of a spiritually free person.[22] Internally, such a person is utterly unselfish, free from fear and expectations, and filled with peace and contentment. These characteristics manifest externally through a calm and cheerful personality, unflappable during crises, forbearing in difficult situations, wise in taking the right decisions, and ever ready to help in whatever way possible.

Which is not to suggest that it is easy to recognize an
enlightened being. Oftentimes it is not. Appearances can
be deceptive. Since it's not difficult to maintain a facade
for a while, a person who claims to be enlightened may
not really be. On the other hand, one who makes no
such claim may well be enlightened. After all, what is
the need to trumpet one's enlightenment? Recognizing
an enlightened person can be tricky, since at first glance
some of them may seem to be a bit strange or
unbelievably childlike or, hold your breath, even crazy.
Nevertheless, the characteristics of an enlightened being
cannot remain hidden for long. Anyone who has
watched a person from close quarters for a sustained
length of time knows better. Sooner or later, what is
inside cannot but express itself *outside* through the way a
person speaks, does work and forges relationships.

The texts take the trouble to repeatedly remind us of the
characteristics of the enlightened because they *want* us
to be enlightened. This raises a question: What good will
it do for the unenlightened me to know how enlightened
people live? The answer is simple: If I know how they
live, I can try to live like them myself. The *characteristics*
of the enlightened become the *disciplines* to be practiced
by those seeking enlightenment.[23] After living for a few
years in one of our Vedanta monasteries, a novice once
asked an elderly monk, "What more do I need to do in
order to become enlightened?" The monk's reply was:
"What are you waiting for? Why don't you try to live as
if you are already enlightened?"

It is, of course, natural for an enlightened person to live like an enlightened person. But for an unenlightened person to live *as if* she or he is enlightened is far from easy. It requires enormous effort, similar to the effort the hunter's son had to make to live like a prince that he really was. Like it or not, there's going to be repeated failure in living up to the demands of an enlightened life. Nevertheless, if I persist in my efforts, undaunted by failures, I'll begin to experience periods of success.

In the beginning I may be able to live like an enlightened being for only a few minutes at a stretch. But gradually this period will increase. With practice, when my self-forgetfulness becomes less, I'll dwell with the Ātman identity for longer periods with greater ease and be comfortable with my new identity. When this process reaches its culmination, when I never ever forget that I am the Ātman, the sun of knowledge will have arisen, never ever to set again.[24]

WHEN THE SUN RISES

No matter how long the night, eventually the sun must rise, as it surely does. The wandering of the deluded Ātman from one form to another feels like going round in circles because it is seemingly endless. "Seemingly" is the keyword. For, the circle is no circle when what keeps it going evaporates into thin air. Ignorance powers the circular movement. When knowledge enters the scene, ignorance disappears along with its fabricated looping world.

When I experience my true identity as the Ātman, my body/mind identity disappears. All that I had sought for, consciously or unconsciously, then becomes a reality. Space is overcome when I know that my existence is not limited to this body which I foolishly called my own. Time is overcome when I live in the present, not troubled by the past and not worried about the future. Causality is overcome when I know that I am free, dependent on nothing. Freedom, perfection and bliss are no longer goals to reach at some undetermined time through some undetermined process. I don't have to die in order to be free and perfect. I don't have to die in order to be in heaven. Whatever is promised in heaven becomes my own, here and now.

Such is the power of knowledge! The good news is that knowledge is always with me. The bad news is that I can't access it until the covering of ignorance is removed. This is accomplished through the practice of jñāna yoga. Once the cover of ignorance is blown, the ever-present light of knowledge shines forth. It's like the bright rays of the sun illuminating the landscape when the dark covering of clouds has dissipated.[25]

Bathed in the light of consciousness which is my own— more accurately, which *is* me—I discover that I am present everywhere and nowhere. I know everything and nothing. I am everyone and no one. I am no longer I because you are no longer you. The distinction between "I" and "you," the difference between "this" and "that," vanishes. All is one and one is all.[26] The sun has risen.

NOTES

PREFACE

1. See Swami Atmarupananda, "The Continuing Development of the *Complete Works*," *Vedanta Kesari* (December 2013), 469.
2. "Discourses on Jnana Yoga" were originally recorded by Vivekananda's disciple S. E. Waldo. Swami Saradananda copied them from her notebook in 1896. As found in volume 8 of the *Complete Works*, these discourses can be subdivided into two parts: sections I through VII (p. 3–27) are from Jnana Yoga classes given in New York City. Sections VII through IX (p. 27–35) are notes from classes at Thousand Island Park in upstate New York. The fuller version of the Thousand Island Park class notes forms "Inspired Talks."
3. CW, 5. 304.
4. Depending on the context, "Ātman" also has different connotations in Sanskrit texts. But in this book I use the word "Ātman" to refer to the nonmaterial core of our being.

1. KNOWLEDGE

1. *Muṇḍaka Upaniṣad*, 1.1.2.
2. The eyes are only doors to the real sense of vision: "The eyes are not the organs. They are but the instruments of vision, and behind them is the real organ, the nerve centre in the brain. If that centre be injured, a man may have the clearest pair of eyes, yet he will not be able to see anything. ... Thus, with all our senses." CW, 2. 213–14. See also CW, 2. 265–66.
3. "Knowledge is mere classification. When we find many things of the same kind we call the sum of them by a certain name and are satisfied; we discover 'facts,' never 'why.' We take a circuit in a wider field of darkness and think we know something!" CW, 7. 18.
4. "All knowledge is inherent in us. Nothing comes from 'outside.' ... What we say a man 'knows,' should, in strict psychological language, be what he 'discovers' or 'unveils' ... All knowledge that

the world has ever received comes from the mind; the infinite
library of the universe is in your own mind. The external world is
simply the suggestion, the occasion, which sets you to study your
own mind, but the object of your study is always your own mind.
The falling of an apple gave the suggestion to Newton, and he
studied his own mind. He rearranged all the previous links of
thought in his mind and discovered a new link among them, which
we call the law of gravitation." CW, 1. 28.

5. "The human mind naturally wants to get outside, to peer out of
the body, as it were, through the channels of the organs. The eye
must see, the ear must hear, the senses must sense the external
world—and naturally the beauties and sublimities of nature
captivate our attention. The first questions that arose in the human
soul were about the external world. The solution of the mystery
was asked of the sky, of the stars, of the heavenly bodies, of the
earth, of the rivers, of the mountains, of the ocean; and in all
ancient religions we find traces of how the groping human mind at
first caught at everything external." CW, 2. 212.

6. "As the question went deeper and deeper, these external
manifestations failed to satisfy the human mind, and finally the
energy turned inward, and the question was asked of one's own
soul. From the macrocosm the question was reflected back to the
microcosm; from the external world the question was reflected to
the internal. From analyzing the external nature, we are led to
analyze the internal; this questioning of the internal nature comes
with a higher state of civilization, with a deeper insight into nature,
with a higher state of growth." CW, 2. 212.

7. "You as reality are unknown and unknowable. You are x and you
act upon my mind, and the mind throws a wave in the direction
from which the impact comes, and that wave is what I call Mr. or
Mrs. So-and-so. There are two elements in the perception, one
coming from outside and the other from inside, and the
combination of these two, $x +$ mind, is our external universe. All
knowledge is by reaction. In the case of a whale it has been
determined by calculation how long after its tail is struck, its mind
reacts and the whale feels the pain. Similar is the case with internal
perception. The real self within me is also unknown and
unknowable. Let us call it y. When I know myself as so-and-so, it is
$y +$ the mind. That y strikes a blow on the mind. So our whole
world is $x +$ mind (external), and $y +$ mind (internal), x and y
standing for the thing-in-itself behind the external and the internal
worlds respectively." CW, 2. 458.

8. "'This Atman is not to be realized by the power of speech, nor by a vast intellect, nor by the study of the Vedas.' This is a very bold utterance. ... In India the idea is that things exist because they are in the Vedas. In and through the Vedas the whole creation has come. All that is called knowledge is in the Vedas. Every word is sacred and eternal, eternal as the soul, without beginning and without end. The whole of the Creator's mind is in this book, as it were. That is the light in which the Vedas are held. ... In spite of that, look at the boldness of these sages who proclaimed that the truth is not to be found by much study of the Vedas." CW, 2. 169

    "Books cannot teach God, but they can destroy ignorance; their action is negative. To hold to the books and at the same time open the way to freedom is Śaṅkara's great achievement. ... The very books are a part of the ignorance they help to dispel. Their duty is to drive out the ignorance that has come upon knowledge." CW, 7. 53.

9. "Relative knowledge is good because it leads to absolute knowledge. But neither the knowledge of the senses, nor of the mind, nor even of the Vedas is absolute, since they are all within the realm of relative knowledge." CW, 7. 33.

10. Which may have prompted Śaunaka's question, quoted earlier, from the *Muṇḍaka Upaniṣad* (1.1.3): "Tell me, Master, what is that knowing which everything becomes known?"

11. "The knowers of brahman say that two kinds of knowledge must be known: lower knowledge and higher knowledge. Of these two, lower knowledge is the Ṛk-veda, the Yajur-veda, the Sāma-veda, the Atharva-veda, phonetics, rituals, grammar, etymology, metre, and astronomy." *Muṇḍaka Upaniṣad*, 1.1.4–5.

12. "The higher knowledge is that through which the imperishable reality is revealed." *Muṇḍaka Upaniṣad*, 1.1.5.

13. "The Self-existent Being hurt the senses by making them extroverted. That is why we perceive only outer objects, not the inner Ātman. But a calm person, seeking immortality, beholds the inner Ātman with the senses turned inward." *Kaṭha Upaniṣad*, 2.1.1.

14. "Here I stand and if I shut my eyes, and try to conceive my existence, 'I,' 'I,' 'I,' what is the idea before me? The idea of a body. Am I, then, nothing but a combination of material substances? The Vedas declare, 'No.' I am a spirit living in a body. I am not the body. The body will die, but I shall not die. Here am I in this body; it will fall, but I shall go on living." CW, 1. 7–8.

15. "The external body perishes in a few years; any simple cause may disturb and destroy it. The finer body is not so easily perishable; yet it sometimes degenerates, and at other times becomes strong. We

see how, in the old man, the mind loses its strength, how, when the
body is vigorous, the mind becomes vigorous, how various
medicines and drugs affect it, how everything external acts on it,
and how it reacts on the external world. Just as the body has its
progress and decadence, so also has the mind." CW, 2. 214–15.

16. "As we proceed we shall find how intimately the mind is connected
with the body. If we believe that the mind is simply a finer part of
the body, and that mind acts upon the body, then it stands to
reason that the body must react upon the mind. If the body is sick,
the mind becomes sick also. If the body is healthy, the mind
remains healthy and strong. When one is angry, the mind becomes
disturbed. Similarly when the mind is disturbed, the body also
becomes disturbed." CW, 1. 132.

17. "A self-luminous existence, independent of any other existence,
could never have been the outcome of anything. It always existed;
there was never a time when it did not exist, because if the soul did
not exist, where was time? Time is in the soul; it is when the soul
reflects its powers on the mind and the mind thinks, that time
comes. When there was no soul, certainly there was no thought,
and without thought, there was no time. How can the soul,
therefore, be said to be existing in time, when time itself exists in
the soul?" CW, 2. 217.

18. "The Atman is the only existence in the human body which is
immaterial. Because it is immaterial, it cannot be a compound, and
because it is not a compound, it does not obey the law of cause and
effect, and so it is immortal. That which is immortal can have no
beginning because everything with a beginning must have an end.
It also follows that it must be formless; there cannot be any form
without matter." CW, 2. 254.

19. "The senses are the horses, the mind is the rein, the intellect is the
charioteer, the Ātman is the rider, and the body is the chariot. The
master of the household—the king, the Ātman—is sitting in this
chariot. If the horses are very strong and do not obey the rein, if
the charioteer (intellect) does not know how to control the horses,
then the chariot (body) will come to grief. But if the horses (senses)
are well controlled and if the rein (mind) is well held in the hands
of the charioteer, the chariot reaches the goal." CW, 1. 235. See
Katha Upaniṣad, 1.3.3–8.

20. See Gītā 2.22, 2.30, 5.13, 14.20.

21. *Katha Upaniṣad*, 1.3.3–8.

22. The "sustained-by-food self" is the body. The "filled-with-life self"
is the life-force (*prāṇa*), which keeps the body alive. The "mental
self" is the repository of thoughts, memories and feelings. The

"knowledgeable self" is the ego as agent (*kartā*), because no acquisition of knowledge is possible without the sense of agency. The "blissful self" is the ego as experiencer (*bhoktā*). This is the only layer active in deep sleep and, since the experience then is of bliss, the layer is called blissful self.

23. Sri Ramakrishna narrated a story to illustrate the point: "The king lives beyond seven gates. At each gate sits a man endowed with great power and glory. At each gate the visitor asks, 'Is this the king?' The gatekeeper answers, 'No. Not this, not this.' The visitor passes through the seventh gate and becomes overpowered with joy. He is speechless. This time he doesn't have to ask, 'Is this the king?' The mere sight of him removes all doubts." *The Gospel of Sri Ramakrishna* (Chennai: Sri Ramakrishna Math, 1980), 218.

24. "Life" may sometimes seem to last a bit longer until the heart stops beating. Death is now understood to be a series of physical events, and distinction is made between cessation of brain activity and cessation of blood circulation and breathing, which has given rise to terms like legal death and clinical death.

25. "The different philosophies seem to agree that the Ātman, whatever it be, has neither form nor shape, and that which has neither form nor shape must be omnipresent. Time begins with mind, space also is in the mind. Causation cannot stand without time. Without the idea of succession there cannot be any idea of causation. Time, space and causation, therefore, are in the mind, and as the Ātman is beyond the mind and formless, it must be beyond time, beyond space, and beyond causation. Now, if it is beyond time, space, and causation, it must be infinite." CW, 2. 78.

26. "There are two parties. One says that there is no soul, that the idea of soul is a delusion produced by the repeated transit of particles of matter, bringing about the combination which you call the body or the brain; that the impression of freedom is the result of the vibrations and motions and continuous transit of these particles.... The other party states that in the rapid succession of thought, matter occurs as a delusion, and does not really exist. So we see one side claiming that spirit is a delusion, and the other, that matter is a delusion. Which side will you take?" CW, 2. 197.

27. Like all Vedanta teachers before him, Vivekananda did not identify the mind with the brain. See, for instance: "Work, but let not the action or the thought produce a deep impression on the mind. Let the ripples come and go, let huge actions proceed from the muscles and the brain, but let them not make any deep impression on the mind." CW, 1. 56.

"Be unattached. Let things work, let brain centers work. Work incessantly, but let not a ripple conquer the mind. Work as if you were a stranger in this land, a sojourner. Work incessantly, but do not bind yourselves. Bondage is terrible." CW, 1. 56.

28. See Evan Thompson, *Waking, Dreaming, Being: Self and Consciousness in Neuroscience, Meditation, and Philosophy* (New York: Columbia University Press, 2015), 101–102.

29. "The Ātman is indeed Brahman." *Bṛhadāraṇyaka Upaniṣad*, 4.4.5. "Brahman is consciousness." *Aitareya Upaniṣad*, 3.1.3.

30. "It is through the Self that you know anything. I see the chair; but to see the chair, I have first to perceive myself and then the chair. It is in and through the Self that the chair is perceived. It is in and through the Self that you are known to me, that the whole world is known to me; and therefore to say this Self is unknown is sheer nonsense. Take off the Self and the whole universe vanishes. In and through the Self all knowledge comes. Therefore it is the best known of all." CW, 2. 305.

31. "This chair is known, but God is intensely more than that, because in and through Him we have to know this chair itself. He is the Witness, the eternal Witness of all knowledge. Whatever we know we have to know in and through Him. He is the Essence of our own Self. He is the Essence of this ego, this I, and we cannot know anything excepting in and through that I. Therefore you have to know everything in and through Brahman. To know the chair you have to know it in and through God. Thus God is infinitely nearer to us than the chair, but yet He is infinitely higher. Neither known, nor unknown, but something infinitely higher than either. He is your Self." CW, 2. 133.

32. "Never was seen any gross matter which had intelligence as its own essence. No dull or dead matter can illumine itself. It is intelligence that illumines all matter. This hall is here only through intelligence because, as a hall, its existence would be unknown unless some intelligence built it. This body is not self-luminous; if it were, it would be so in a dead man also. Neither can the mind be self-luminous. It is not of the essence of intelligence. That which is self-luminous cannot decay. The luminosity of that which shines through a borrowed light comes and goes; but that which is light itself, what can make that come and go, flourish and decay? We see that the moon waxes and wanes, because it shines through the borrowed light of the sun. If a lump of iron is put into the fire and made red-hot, it glows and shines, but its light will vanish, because it is borrowed. So, decadence is possible only of that light which is borrowed and is not of its own essence." CW, 2. 215.

2. IGNORANCE

1. "Maya cannot be said to exist. Form cannot be said to exist, because it depends upon the existence of another thing. It cannot be said as not to exist, seeing that it makes all this difference." CW, 2. 275-76. See also Śaṅkarācārya, *Vivekacūḍāmaṇi*, 109.

2. "Māyā is not a theory for the explanation of the world; it is simply a statement of facts as they exist, that the very basis of our being is contradiction, that wherever there is good, there must also be evil, and wherever there is evil, there must be some good, wherever there is life, death must follow as its shadow, and everyone who smiles will have to weep, and vice versa. Nor can this state of things be remedied. We may verily imagine that there will be a place where there will be only good and no evil, where we shall only smile and never weep. This is impossible in the nature of things; for the conditions will remain the same. Wherever there is the power of producing a smile in us, there lurks the power of producing tears. Wherever there is the power of producing happiness, there lurks somewhere the power of making us miserable." CW, 2. 97.

3. "Every child is a born optimist; he dreams golden dreams. In youth he becomes still more optimistic. It is hard for a young man to believe that there is such a thing as death, such a thing as defeat or degradation. Old age comes, and life is a mass of ruins. Dreams have vanished into the air, and the man becomes a pessimist. Thus we go from one extreme to another, buffeted by nature, without knowing where we are going." CW, 2. 91-92.

    "We are all after the Golden Fleece. Every one of us thinks that this will be his. Every reasonable man sees that his chance is, perhaps, one in twenty millions, yet everyone struggles for it. And this is māyā." CW, 2. 93. See also CW, 2. 118.

4. "The whole world is going towards death; everything dies. All our progress, our vanities, our reforms, our luxuries, our wealth, our knowledge, have that one end—death. That is all that is certain. Cities come and go, empires rise and fall, planets break into pieces and crumble into dust, to be blown about by the atmospheres of other planets. Thus it has been going on from time without beginning. Death is the end of everything. Death is the end of life, of beauty, of wealth, of power, of virtue too. Saints die and sinners die, kings die and beggars die. They are all going to death, and yet this tremendous clinging on to life exists. Somehow, we do not know why, we cling to life; we cannot give it up. And this is māyā." CW, 2. 92-93.

5. "The mother is nursing a child with great care; all her soul, her life, is in that child. The child grows, becomes a man, and perchance becomes a blackguard and a brute, kicks her and beats her every day; and yet the mother clings to the child; and when her reason awakes, she covers it up with the idea of love. She little thinks that it is not love, that it is something which has got hold of her nerves, which she cannot shake off; however she may try, she cannot shake off the bondage she is in. And this is māyā." CW, 2. 93. See also CW, 2. 119–20.

6. "There is this contradiction in knowledge. It seems that man can know everything, if he only wants to know; but before he has gone a few steps, he finds an adamantine wall which he cannot pass. All his work is in a circle, and he cannot go beyond that circle. The problems which are nearest and dearest to him are impelling him on and calling, day and night, for a solution, but he cannot solve them, because he cannot go beyond his intellect. And yet that desire is implanted strongly in him." CW, 2. 91. See also CW, 2. 119.

7. "Time, the avenger of everything, comes, and nothing is left. He swallows up the saint and the sinner, the king and the peasant, the beautiful and the ugly; he leaves nothing. Everything is rushing towards that one goal, destruction. Our knowledge, our arts, our sciences, everything is rushing towards it. None can stem the tide, none can hold it back for a minute. We may try to forget it, in the same way that persons in a plague-stricken city try to create oblivion by drinking, dancing, and other vain attempts, and so becoming paralyzed. So we are trying to forget, trying to create oblivion by all sort of sense-pleasures. And this is māyā." CW, 2. 121. See also Bhartṛhari's *Vairāgya Śatakam,* 7.

8. "The māyā of Vedanta, in its last developed form, is neither Idealism nor Realism, nor is it a theory. It is a simple statement of facts—what we are and what we see around us." CW, 2.89. See also 2.97, 2.105.

9. How the "ridiculous" became "normal," or how the impossible became seemingly possible, even "natural," is brilliantly described by Śrī Śaṅkarācārya at the beginning of his commentary on the *Brahma Sūtra.*

10. "Devotion to ceremonials, satisfaction in the senses, and forming various theories, have drawn a veil between ourselves and truth. This 'veil' is the real explanation of Vedanta: the truth was there all the time, it was only this veil that had covered it." CW, 1. 355.

11. "How can you see your own Self ? You can only reflect yourself. So all this universe is the reflection of that one eternal Being, the

Ātman, and as the reflection falls upon good or bad reflectors, so good or bad images are cast up. Thus in the murderer, the reflector —not the Self—is bad. In the saint the reflector is pure. The Self, or the Ātman, is by its own nature pure. It is the same, the one existence of the universe that is reflecting itself from the lowest worm to the highest and most perfect being. The whole of this universe is one unity, one existence, physically, mentally, morally and spiritually. We are looking upon this one existence in different forms and creating all these images upon It. To the being who has limited himself to the condition of man, it appears as the world of man. To the being who is on a higher plane of existence, it may seem like heaven." CW, 2. 249.

12. "It is this universe which, from the human plane, is seen as the earth, the sun, the moon, the stars, and all such things—it is this very universe which, seen from the plane of wickedness, appears as a place of punishment. And this very universe is seen as heaven by those who want to see it as heaven." CW, 2. 278.

13. "Everyone's idea of pleasure is different. ... Our pleasures are always changing. If a young man dreams of heaven, he dreams of a heaven where he will have a beautiful wife. When that same man becomes old he does not want a wife. It is our necessities which make our heaven, and the heaven changes with the change of our necessities." CW, 2. 165–66.

14. "Space-time-causation (*deśa-kāla-nimitta*), or name and form (*nāma-rūpa*), is what is called māyā." CW, 5. 336.

15. According to Vedanta, "the mind is limited, it cannot go beyond certain limits—beyond time, space, and causation. As no man can jump out of his own self, so no man can go beyond the limits that have been put upon him by the laws of time and space. Every attempt to solve the laws of causation, time, and space would be futile, because the very attempt would have to be made by taking for granted the existence of these three." CW, 2. 90-91.

16. "What you call matter, or spirit, or mind, or anything else you may like to call them, the fact remains the same: we cannot say that they are, we cannot say that they are not. We cannot say they are one, we cannot say they are many. This eternal play of light and darkness—indiscriminate, indistinguishable, inseparable—is always there. A fact, yet at the same time not a fact; awake and at the same time asleep. This is a statement of facts, and this is what is called māyā." CW, 2. 112.

17. "It is statement of fact that this world is a Tantalus's hell, that we do not know anything about this universe, yet at the same time we cannot say that we do not know. I cannot say that this chain

exists, when I think that I do not know it. It may be an entire delusion of my brain. I may be dreaming all the time. I am dreaming that I am talking to you, and that you are listening to me. No one can prove that it is not a dream. My brain itself may be a dream, and as to that no one has ever seen his own brain. We all take it for granted. So it is with everything. My own body I take for granted. At the same time I cannot say, I do not know. This standing between knowledge and ignorance, this mystic twilight, the mingling of truth and falsehood—and where they meet—no one knows. We are walking in the midst of a dream, half sleeping, half waking, passing all our lives in a haze; this is the fate of everyone of us. This is the fate of all sense-knowledge. This is the fate of all philosophy, of all boasted science, of all boasted human knowledge. This is the universe." CW, 2. 111-12.

18. "The real person, therefore, is one and infinite, the omnipresent spirit. And the apparent person is only a limitation of that real person. In that sense the mythologies are true that the apparent person, however great he or she may be, is only a dim reflection of the real person who is beyond. The real person, the spirit, being beyond cause and effect, not bound by time and space, must, therefore, be free. The spirit was never bound and could not be bound. The apparent person, the reflection, is limited by time, space, and causation, and is therefore bound." CW, 2. 78.

19. "The whole of the Vedanta philosophy is in this story: Two birds of golden plumage sat on the same tree. The one above, serene, majestic, immersed in his own glory; the one below restless and eating the fruits of the tree, now sweet, now bitter. Once he ate an exceptionally bitter fruit, then he paused and looked up at the majestic bird above; but he soon forgot about the other bird and went on eating the fruits of the tree as before. Again he ate a bitter fruit, and this time he hopped up a few boughs nearer to the bird at the top. This happened many times until at last the lower bird came to the place of the upper bird and lost himself. He found all at once that there had never been two birds, but that he was all the time that upper bird, serene, majestic, and immersed in his own glory." CW, 7. 80. See also CW, 2. 394-95 and 8. 4-5. See *Mundaka Upaniṣad*, 3.1.1-2.

3. DISCERNMENT

1. "It is reason that develops into inspiration, and therefore inspiration does not contradict reason, but fulfills it. Things which reason cannot get at are brought to light by inspiration; and they do not contradict reason. The old man does not contradict the child, but fulfills the child. Therefore you must always bear in mind that the great danger lies in mistaking the lower form of instrument to be the higher. Many times instinct is presented before the world as inspiration, and then come all the spurious claims for the gift of prophecy. A fool or a semi-lunatic thinks that the confusion going on in his brain is inspiration, and he wants others to follow him. The most contradictory irrational nonsense that has been preached in the world is simply the instinctive jargon of confused lunatic brains trying to pass for the language of inspiration." CW, 2. 390.

2. See Śaṅkarācārya's commentary on the *Kaṭha Upaniṣad*, 1.3.10.

3. "A stone falls and we ask, why? This question is possible only on the supposition that nothing happens without a cause. I request you to make this very clear in your minds, for whenever we ask why anything happens, we are taking for granted that everything that happens must have a why, that is to say, it must have been preceded by something else which acted as the cause. This precedence and succession are what we call the law of causation.... We shall see later on what Vedanta has to say about it. But first we have to understand this that the very asking of the question 'why' presupposes that everything around us has been preceded by certain things and will be succeeded by certain other things. The other belief involved in this question is that nothing in the universe is independent, that everything is acted upon by something outside itself." CW, 2. 131-32.

4. "It is good to be born in a church, but it is bad to die there. It is good to be born a child, but bad to remain a child. Churches, ceremonies, and symbols are good for children, but when the child is grown, he must burst the church or himself. We must not remain children for ever." CW, 1. 325.

5. "[True religion] is not talk, or doctrines, or theories; nor is it sectarianism ... Religion does not consist in erecting temples, or building churches, or attending public worship. It is not to be found in books, or in words, or in lectures, or in organizations. Religion consists in realization." CW, 4. 179-80.

   "[We] must realize God, feel God, see God, talk to God. That is religion." CW, 4. 165.

6. "When we speak of the universe, we only mean that portion of existence which is limited by our mind—the universe of the senses, which we can see, feel, touch, hear, think of, imagine. This alone is under law; but beyond it existence cannot be subject to law, because causation does not extend beyond the world of our minds." CW, 1. 95.

7. "Here are two Sanskrit words. The one is *pravṛtti*, which means revolving towards, and the other is *nivṛtti*, which means revolving away. The 'revolving towards' is what we call the world, the 'I and mine;' it includes all those things which are always enriching that 'me' by wealth and money and power, and name and fame, and which are of a grasping nature, always tending to accumulate everything in one centre, that centre being 'myself.'" CW, 1. 85–86.

8. "No two people see the same world." CW, 7. 74.

9. "Some people, who begin by saying that the world is a hell, often end by saying that it is a heaven when they succeed in the practice of self-control." CW, 1. 92.

10. "The wicked see this universe as a hell, and the partially good see it as heaven, while the perfect beings realize it as God himself." CW, 2. 279.

    "Change the subject, and the object is bound to change; purify yourself, and the world is bound to be purified. This one thing requires to be taught now more than ever before. We are becoming more and more busy about our neighbors, and less and less about ourselves. The world will change if we change; if we are pure, the world will become pure. The question is why I should see evil in others. I cannot see evil unless I be evil." CW, 1. 426.

11. "How do you prove the world? Its only proof is that we all see it and feel it." CW, 7. 48.

12. One possible objection here is this: while the waking world remains one and the same, the dream world changes every night. A little bit of discernment will convince us that this objection doesn't hold. In my dream I have no awareness that this is a "new" world that I am seeing. It feels like the same old world that I am used to—an experience identical with what we feel when we are awake.

    It is possible, therefore, to encounter a different world in every dream and not know it to be "new." In the same way, it is possible to encounter a different world when we wake up and yet believe it to be the same old world that I had seen before falling asleep.

    What all this drives us toward is the inevitable conclusion that *both* are dreams, the waking-dream and the dream-dream. Even deep sleep is a dream, which is why the *Aitareya Upaniṣad* (1.3.12) says that there are three kinds of dreams. Whenever we perceive something that is not real, what else could it be but a "dream"?

13. "What does the statement of the existence of the world mean, then? 'This world has no existence.' What is meant by that? It means that it has no absolute existence. It exists only in relation to my mind, to your mind, and to the mind of everyone else. We see this world with the five senses but if we had another sense, we would see in it something more. If we had yet another sense, it would appear as something still different. It has therefore no real existence; it has no unchangeable, immovable, infinite existence. Nor can it be called nonexistence, seeing that it exists, and we have to work in and through it. It is a mixture of existence and nonexistence." CW, 2. 91.

14. "If you have seen a certain country, and a man forces you to say that you have not seen it, still in your heart of hearts you know you have. So when you see religion and God in a more intense sense than you see this external world, nothing will be able to shake your belief. Then you have real faith. That is what is meant by the words in your Gospel, 'He who has faith even as a grain of mustard seed.' Then you will know the Truth because you have become the Truth. This is the watchword of Vedanta—realize religion, no talking will do." CW, 2. 165.

15. His Eastern and Western Disciples, *The Life of Swami Vivekananda*, 2 vols. (Kolkata: Advaita Ashrama, 1979), 1. 77.

16. From a philosophical perspective, the world is nonsignificant (*tuccha*), because it doesn't help in any way to reach the truth. That is why the philosophical inquiry in Vedanta takes a U-turn, recognizes the exploration of the world as a nonstarter, and begins to examine the nature of the Ātman instead.

17. "We see that a human being is composed, first, of an external covering, the body; secondly, the finer body, consisting of mind, intellect, and egoism. Behind them is the real Self. We have seen that all the qualities and powers of the gross body are borrowed from the mind, which in turn borrows its powers and luminosity from the Self." CW, 2. 216.

"First, here is the body, second, the mind, or instrument of thought, and third behind this mind is the Self. The Sanskrit word is Ātman." CW, 2. 233.

According to Vedanta, a human being "consists of three parts — the body, the internal organ or the mind, and behind that, what is called the Ātman, the Self. The body is the external coating and the mind is the internal coating of the Ātman who is the real perceiver, the real enjoyer, the being in the body who is working the body by means of the internal organ or the mind." CW, 2. 254.

18. "It is not that the soul and the mind and the body are three separate existences, for the organism made of these three is really one. It is the same thing which appears as the body, as the mind, and as the thing beyond mind and body, but it is not at the same time all these. He who sees the body does not see the mind even, he who sees the mind does not see that which he calls the soul, and he who sees the soul—for him body and mind have vanished. He who sees only motion never sees absolute calm, and he who sees absolute calm—for him motion has vanished. A rope is taken for a snake. He who sees the rope as the snake, for him the rope has vanished, and when the delusion ceases and he looks at the rope, the snake has vanished." CW, 2. 274. See also 2. 344.

19. "To give an illustration, there is a wave on the ocean. The wave is the same as the ocean certainly, and yet we know it is a wave, and as such different from the ocean. What makes this difference? The name and the form; that is, the idea in the mind and the form. Now, can we think of a wave-form as something separate from the ocean? Certainly not. It is always associated with the ocean idea. If the wave subsides, the form vanishes in a moment, and yet the form was not a delusion. So long as the wave existed the form was there, and you were bound to see the form. This is māyā. ... the Absolute is that ocean while you and I, the suns and the stars, and everything else are various waves of that ocean. And what makes the waves different? Only the form, and that form is time, space, and causation, all entirely dependent on the wave. As soon as the individual gives up this māyā, it vanishes for him and he becomes free." CW, 2. 136.

20. "Everyone and everything is the Ātman—the Self—the sexless, the pure, the ever-blessed. It is the name, the form, the body, which are material, and they make all this difference. If you take away these two differences of name and form, the whole universe is one; there are no two, but one everywhere. You and I are one. There is neither nature, nor God, nor the universe, only that one infinite existence, out of which, through name and form, all these are manufactured... All this universe is the reflection of that one eternal Being, the Ātman." CW, 2. 249.

21. "Vedanta says, you are free and not free at the same time—never free on the earthly plane, but ever free on the spiritual." CW, 7. 32.

22. "What we call the most arrant superstition and the highest philosophy really have a common aim in that they both try to show

the way out of the same difficulty, and in most cases this way is through the help of someone who is not himself bound by the laws of nature, in one word, someone who is free. In spite of all the difficulties and differences of opinion about the nature of the one free agent, whether he is a Personal God, or a sentient being like man, whether masculine, feminine, or neuter—and the discussions have been endless—the fundamental idea is the same." CW, 2. 125.

23. "Seek to know Brahman, from whom all beings are born, in whom they live, and to whom they eventually return." *Taittirīya Upaniṣad*, 3.1.1.

    "Brahman is the source of the origin etc [i.e. sustenance and dissolution] of this world." *Brahma Sūtra*, 1.1.2.

24. *Sarvam khalu idaṁ brahma*, "All this is Brahman." *Chāndogya Upaniṣad*, 3.14.1.

    "Everything that you see, feel, or hear, the whole universe, is God's creation, or to be a little more accurate, is his projection; or to be still more accurate, is the Lord himself. It is he who is shining as the sun and the stars, he is the mother earth. He is the ocean himself. He comes as gentle showers, he is the gentle air that we breathe in, and he it is who is working as force in the body. He is the speech that is uttered, he is the man who is talking. He is the audience that is here. He is the platform on which I stand, he is the light that enables me to see your faces. It is all he. He himself is both the material and the efficient cause of this universe, and he it is that gets involved in the minute cell, and evolves at the other end and becomes God again. He it is that comes down and becomes the lowest atom, and slowly unfolding his nature, rejoins himself. This is the mystery of the universe. 'You are the man, you are the woman, you are the strong man walking in the pride of youth, you are the old man tottering on crutches, you are in everything. You are everything, O Lord.' This is the only solution of the cosmos that satisfies the human intellect. In one word, we are born of him, we live in him, and unto him we return." CW, 2. 211.

25. "So long as I say 'you,' I have the right to speak of God protecting us. When I see another, I must take all the consequences and put in the third, the ideal, which stands between us; that is the apex of the triangle. The vapor becomes snow, then water, then Ganga; but when it is vapor, there is no Ganga, and when it is water, we think of no vapor in it. The idea of creation or change is inseparably connected with will. So long as we perceive this world in motion, we have to conceive will behind it." CW, 7. 57.

26. "In worshiping God we have been always worshiping our own hidden Self." CW, 2. 279.

27. "Manifoldness is only apparent. Man is only apparently a person, but in reality he is the impersonal Being. God is a person only apparently, but really he is the impersonal Being." CW, 2. 192.

28. "The Ātman, the perceiver of everything, is Brahman." *Bṛhadāraṇyaka Upaniṣad*, 2.5.19. "The Ātman is indeed Brahman." *Bṛhadāraṇyaka Upaniṣad*, 4.4.5.

29. "The soul is a circle whose circumference is nowhere (limitless), but whose center is in some body. Death is but a change of center. God is a circle whose circumference is nowhere, and whose center is everywhere." CW, 5. 271.

30. "Religion permeates the whole of our life, not only the present, but the past, present and future. It is, therefore, the eternal relation between the eternal soul and the eternal God." CW, 3. 4.

31. "Teach yourselves, teach every one his real nature, call upon the sleeping soul and see how it awakes. Power will come, glory will come, goodness will come, purity will come, and everything that is excellent will come when this sleeping soul is roused to self-conscious activity." CW, 3. 193.

32. "We see this universe as human beings, and our God is our human explanation of the universe. Suppose a cow were philosophical and had religion, it would have a cow universe, and a cow solution of the problem, and it would not be possible that it should see our God. Suppose cats became philosophers, they would see a cat universe and have a cat solution of the problem of the universe, and a cat ruling it. So we see from this that our explanation of the universe is not the whole of the solution." CW, 2. 155.

33. "The great mistake is in recognizing the evolution of the worshipers, while we do not acknowledge the evolution of the Worshiped. God is not credited with the advance that his devotees have made. That is to say, you and I, as representing ideas, have grown; these gods also, as representing ideas, have grown. This may seem somewhat curious to you—that God can grow. He cannot. He is unchangeable. But our ideas of God are constantly changing and expanding.... The idea that we form of God is a mere manifestation, our own creation. Behind that is the real God who never changes, the ever pure, the immutable. But the manifestation is always changing, revealing the reality behind more and more. When it reveals more of the fact behind, it is called progression; when it hides more of the fact behind, it is called retrogression. Thus, as we grow, so the gods grow. From the

ordinary point of view, just as we reveal ourselves as we evolve, so the gods reveal themselves." CW, 2. 107.

34. "We do not manufacture God out of our own brains; but we can only see God in the light of our own capacity, and we attribute to God the best of all we know. Each attribute is the whole of God, and this signifying the whole by one quality is the metaphysical explanation of the personal God. God is without form, yet has all forms; God is without qualities, yet has all qualities. As human beings, we have to see the trinity of existence—God, human beings, nature; and we cannot do otherwise." CW, 7. 82.

35. "The idea that the goal is far off, far beyond nature, attracting us all towards it, has to be brought nearer and nearer, without degrading or degenerating it. The God of heaven becomes the God in nature, and the God in nature becomes the God who is nature, and the God who is nature becomes the God within this temple of the body, and the God dwelling in the temple of the body at last becomes the temple itself, becomes the soul and human being—and there it reaches the last words it can teach. He whom the sages have been seeking in all these places is in our own hearts; the voice that you heard was right, says the Vedanta, but the direction you gave to the voice was wrong. That ideal of freedom that you perceived was correct, but you projected it outside yourself, and that was your mistake. Bring it nearer and nearer, until you find that it was all the time within you, it was the Self of your own self." CW, 2. 128.

"These are the salient points of the three steps which Indian religious thought has taken in regard to God. We have seen that it began with the personal, the extra-cosmic God. It went from the external to the internal cosmic body, God immanent in the universe, and ended in identifying the soul itself with God…. This is the last word of the Vedas. It begins with dualism, goes through a qualified monism and ends in perfect monism." CW, 2. 252.

"Personal God comes nearer and nearer until he melts away, and there is no more personal God and no more 'I', all is merged in Self." CW, 7. 58.

36. Both the dream world and the waking world are results of forgetfulness. A dream is possible only in sleep when we become forgetful of our waking identity. The perception of the world is possible only when we become forgetful of our Ātman identity due to ignorance. This is another reason the two are comparable.

37. "The whole life is a succession of dreams. My ambition is to be a conscious dreamer, that is all." CW, 5. 100.

38. See *Aitareya Upaniṣad*, 1.3.12.

39. "When the mind is in a particular condition it sees a certain vision, dreams a certain dream. So in this condition, we are all seeing this world and man and animals and all these things. But in this very place, this condition will change. And the very thing we are seeing as earth, we shall see as heaven, or we may see it as the opposite place or as any place we like. All this depends on our desires.... Two things exist in the world—dream and reality. What we call life is a succession of dreams—dream within dream. One dream is called heaven, another earth, another hell, and so on. One dream is called the human body, another the animal body, and so on—all are dreams. The reality is what is called Brahman, that Being who is Existence, Knowledge, Bliss." CW, 9. 242–43.

40. "Brahman is reality (satya), knowledge (jñāna), and infinity (ananta)," according to Taittirīya Upaniṣad, 2.1. The Chāndogya Upaniṣad, 7.23.1, points out that real joy is to be found only in the infinite, never in what is finite. That is how God, being infinite, is identified with real joy or bliss (ānanda).

41. "What the world wants today is twenty men and women who can dare to stand in the street yonder, and say that they possess nothing but God. Who will go? Why should one fear? If this is true, what else could matter? If it is not true, what do our lives matter?" CW, 8. 261.

42. "Recognizing the distinction between guṇa and karma, a person knows that guṇas as senses merely interact with guṇas as objects, and so does not become attached." Gītā, 3. 28.

4. PRACTICE

1. "How has all the knowledge in the world been gained but by the concentration of the powers of the mind? The world is ready to give up its secrets if we only know how to knock, how to give it the necessary blow. The strength and force of the blow come through concentration. There is no limit to the power of the human mind. The more concentrated it is, the more power is brought to bear on one point; that is the secret." CW, 1. 130–31.

2. "The object of jñāna yoga is the same as that of bhakti and rāja yogas, but the method is different. This is the yoga for the strong, for those who are neither mystical nor devotional, but rational. As the bhakti yogī works his way to complete oneness with the Supreme through love and devotion, so the jñāna yogī forces his way to the realization of God by the power of pure reason. He must be prepared to throw away all old idols, all old beliefs and

superstitions, all desire for this world or another, and be
determined only to find freedom." CW, 8. 3.

3.   "Jñāna yoga is divided into three parts. First: hearing the truth—
that the Ātman is the only reality and that everything else is māyā.
Second: reasoning upon this philosophy from all points of view.
Third: giving up all further argumentation and realizing the truth."
CW, 8. 154-155.

4.   "Everything is evanescent. Enjoyment, misery, luxury, wealth,
power, and poverty, even life itself, are all evanescent." CW, 2. 71.

5.   "Meditating on the reality always and reminding oneself of its real
nature are the only ways in this [jñāna] yoga." CW, 8. 155.

6.   Although *nididhyāsana* of the Upaniṣads and *dhyāna* of the Yoga-
sūtras are both translated as "meditation," there is a subtle
distinction between the two. *Nididhyāsana* needs effort, whereas
dhyāna is effortless—it is an unbroken flow of the mind toward the
object of meditation (See *Yoga Sūtra*, 3.2).

7.   "There is a great tendency in modern times to talk too much of
work and decry thought. Doing is very good, but that comes from
thinking. Little manifestations of energy through the muscles are
called work. But where there is no thought, there will be no work.
Fill the brain, therefore, with high thoughts, highest ideals, place
them day and night before you, and out of that will come great
work." CW, 2. 85-86.

   "Evil thoughts, looked at materially, are the disease bacilli.
Each thought is a little hammer blow on the lump of iron which
our bodies are, manufacturing out of it what we want it to be. We
are heirs to all the good thoughts of the universe, if we open
ourselves to them." CW, 7. 20.

8.   "We are what our thoughts have made us; so take care of what you
think. Words are secondary. Thoughts live, they travel far. Each
thought we think is tinged with our own character, so that for the
pure and holy man, even his jests or abuse will have the twist of his
own love and purity and do good." CW, 7. 14.

9.   "'This Ātman is first to be heard of.' Hear day and night that you
are the Ātman. Repeat it to yourselves day and night till it enters
into your very veins, till it tingles in every drop of blood, till it is in
your flesh and bone. Let the whole body be full of that one ideal, 'I
am the birthless, the deathless, the blissful, the omniscient, the
omnipotent, ever-glorious Ātman.' Think on it day and night;
think on it till it becomes part and parcel of your life. Meditate
upon it, and out of that will come work. 'Out of the fullness of the
heart the mouth speaketh,' and out of the fullness of the heart the
hand worketh also. Action will come. Fill yourselves with the idea;

whatever you do, think well on it. All your actions will be magnified, transformed, deified, by the very power of the thought. If matter is powerful, thought is omnipotent. Bring this thought to bear upon your life, fill yourselves with the thought of your almightiness, your majesty, and your glory." CW, 2. 302.

10. "We see the world as we are. Suppose there is a baby in a room with a bag of gold on the table and a thief comes and steals the gold. Would the baby know it was stolen? That which we have inside, we see outside. The baby has no thief inside and sees no thief outside." CW, 2.87.

11. "*Svastha*, the Sanskrit word for 'standing on your own Self,' is used colloquially in India to inquire, 'Are you well, are you happy?'" CW, 7. 82.

12. "Happiness and misery are states and states must always change. But the nature of the Atman is bliss, peace, unchanging. We have not to get it, we have it already. Only wash away the dross and see it." CW, 7. 11.

13. "Make the heart like an ocean, go beyond all the trifles of the world, be mad with joy even at evil. See the world as a picture and then enjoy its beauty, knowing that nothing affects you." CW, 7. 13.

14. The higher mind is sometimes referred to as *dhī*, and it is the guidance of this higher mind which is sought in the sacred Gāyatrī prayer.

15. Since both the higher mind as well as the lower mind can act as if they were the "self," the Gītā (6.5) refers to them both as self: "The self [mind] should not be weakened, since the self ["lower mind"] has to be uplifted by the self ["higher mind"]. For the self [mind] can be one's friend and the self [mind] can be one's enemy." The next verse points out that the mind becomes one's friend with the practice of self-control. Without it, the mind behaves like one's own enemy.

16. "Religion begins with a tremendous dissatisfaction with the present state of things, with our lives, and a hatred, an intense hatred, for this patching up of life, an unbounded disgust for fraud and lies. He alone can be religious who dares say, as the mighty Buddha once said ... 'Death is better than a vegetating ignorant life; it is better to die on the battlefield than to live a life of defeat.' This is the basis of religion.... This is what the Vedas preach: Be not in despair; the way is very difficult, like walking on the edge of a razor; yet despair not, arise, awake, and find the ideal, the goal." CW, 2. 123-24.

17. "Let positive, strong, helpful thought enter into the brain from very childhood. Lay yourselves open to these thoughts, and not to

weakening and paralyzing ones. Say to your own minds, 'I am He. I am He.' Let it ring day and night in your minds like a song, and at the point of death declare, 'I am He.' That is the Truth; the infinite strength of the world is yours. Drive out the superstition that has covered your minds. Let us be brave. Know the Truth and practice the Truth. The goal may be distant, but awake, arise, and stop not till the goal is reached." CW, 2. 87.

18. यत्रास्ति न माता न पिता न बन्धु: भ्रातापि यत्र सुहृज्जनश्च ।
   न ज्ञायते यत्र दिनं न रात्रि: तत्रात्मदीपं शरणं प्रपद्ये ॥

19. "'Brahman alone is true, all else is false and I am Brahman.' Only by telling ourselves this until we make it a part of our very being, can we rise beyond all duality, beyond both good and evil, pleasure and pain, joy and sorrow, and know ourselves as the One, eternal, unchanging, infinite—the 'One without a second.'" CW, 8. 5.

20. Adapted from an old but undated Sanskrit composition. The "three sorrows" are those caused by the body, by others and by natural disasters. The "three states" are those of waking, dream and deep sleep.

21. Swami Vivekananda paraphrased it as follows: "'I have neither death nor fear, I have neither caste nor creed, I have neither father nor mother nor brother, neither friend nor foe, for I am Existence, Knowledge, and Bliss Absolute; I am the Blissful One, I am the Blissful One. I am not bound either by virtue or vice, by happiness or misery. Pilgrimages and books and ceremonials can never bind me. I have neither hunger nor thirst; the body is not mine, nor am I subject to the superstitions and decay that come to the body, I am Existence, Knowledge, and Bliss Absolute; I am the Blissful One, I am the Blissful One.' This, says the Vedanta, is the only prayer that we should have. This is the only way to reach the goal, to tell ourselves, and to tell everybody else, that we are divine. And as we go on repeating this, strength comes." CW, 2. 202.

22. प्रात: स्मरामि हृदि संस्फुरदात्मतत्त्वं सच्चित्सुखं परमहंसगतिं तुरीयम् ।
   यत्स्वप्नजागरसुषुप्तमवैति नित्यं तद्ब्रह्म निष्कलमहं न च भूतसङ्घ: ॥
   प्रातर्भजामि मनसा वचसामगम्यं वाचो विभान्ति निखिला यदनुग्रहेण ।
   यन्नेतिनेतिवचनैर्निगमा अवोचुस्तं देवदेवमजमच्युतमाहुरग्र्यम् ॥
   प्रातर्नमामि तमस: परमर्कवर्णं पूर्णं सनातनपदं पुरुषोत्तमाख्यम् ।
   यस्मिन्निदं जगदशेषमूतौं रज्ज्यां भुजङ्गम इव प्रतिभासितं वै ॥

23. "Vedanta does not in reality denounce the world. The ideal of renunciation nowhere attains such a height as in the teachings of Vedanta. But, at the same time, dry suicidal advice is not intended; it really means deification of the world—giving up the world as we think of it, as we know it, as it appears to us—and to know what it really is. Deify it; it is God alone. … We have to cover everything

with the Lord himself, not by a false sort of optimism, not by blinding our eyes to the evil, but by really seeing God in everything. Thus we have to give up the world, and when the world is given up, what remains? God. ... In life and in death, in happiness and in misery, the Lord is equally present. The whole world is full of the Lord. Open your eyes and see Him. This is what Vedanta teaches." CW, 2. 146.

24. See Appayā Dīkṣita, *Siddhānta-leśa-saṅgraha*: "āsupteḥ āmṛteḥ kālaṁ nayet vedānta-cintayā."

25. The practice of discernment between the "seen" and the "seer" can be done with the help of the text *Dṛk-Dṛsya-Viveka*.

26. The practice of discernment between the three states can be done with the help of *Māṇḍūkya Upaniṣad*.

27. The practice of discernment between the different layers of my personality can be done with the help of the *Taittirīya Upaniṣad* or the *Vivekacūḍāmaṇi*.

28. *The Gospel of Sri Ramakrishna*, Tr. Swami Nikhilananda (Chennai: Sri Ramakrishna Math), 358.

29. CW, 6. 91–92.

30. "We Vedantists in every difficulty ought to ask the subjective question, 'Why do I see that?'" CW, 8. 383.

31. "This world is like a dog's curly tail, and people have been striving to straighten it out for hundreds of years; but when they let it go, it has curled up again. How could it be otherwise? One must first know how to work without attachment, then one will not be a fanatic. When we know that this world is like a dog's curly tail and will never get straightened, we shall not become fanatics." CW, 1. 79.

32. "Whatever exists in this ever-changing universe must be covered by the Lord." *Īśāvāsyopaniṣad*, 1.

5. ONENESS

1. "Just as by one clod of clay all that is made of clay is known (*vijñātaṁ*), the modification being only a name, arising from speech, and the clay alone is real ..." *Chāndogya Upaniṣad*, 6.1.4.

   "Brahman is consciousness (*prajñānaṁ*)." *Aitareya Upaniṣad*, 3.1.3.

   "The Infinite Being accepts neither the merit nor the demerit of anyone. Knowledge (*jñāna*) is covered by ignorance (*ajñāna*), hence people are deluded." *Gītā*, 5. 15.

2. *Vijñāna* is a derivative of "knowledge" (*vi+jñāna*). The prefix *vi* usually adds specificity or intensity to the word that follows it.

3. "If I know one lump of clay perfectly, I know all the clay there is. This is the knowledge of principles, but their adaptations are various. When you know your Self, you know everything." CW, 5. 411.

4. "Everything is known when the Ātman is experienced through hearing, reflection and meditation." *Bṛhadāraṇyaka Upaniṣad*, 2,4.5, 4.5.6. "The knots of the heart are cut asunder, all doubts are resolved, and all karma is destroyed when the Ātman is experienced fully." *Muṇḍaka Upaniṣad*, 2.2.8. See also *Gītā*, 7.2.

5. Conversation with Swami Bhuteshananda. Belur Math, 1982.

6. "The body and mind are continually changing, and are, in fact, only names of series of changeful phenomena, like rivers whose waters are in a constant state of flux, yet presenting the appearance of unbroken streams." CW, 2. 79.

7. "Menander was a Greco-Bactrian king. He was converted to Buddhism about 150 B.C. by one of the Buddhist missionary monks and was called by them 'Milinda.' He asked a young monk, his teacher, 'Can a perfect man (such as Buddha) be in error or make mistakes?' The young monk's answer was : The perfect man can remain in ignorance of minor matters not in his experience, but he can never be in error as to what his insight has actually realized. He is perfect here and now. He knows the whole mystery, the essence of the universe, but he may not know the mere external variation through which that essence is manifested in time and space. He knows the clay itself, but has not had experience of every shape it may be wrought into. The perfect man knows the Soul itself, but not every form and combination of its manifestation. He would have to attain more relative knowledge just as we do, though on account of his immense power, he would learn it far more quickly." CW, 8. 16–17.

8. "The Ātman cannot be cut, nor burnt, nor wetted, nor dried. Changeless, all-pervading, unmoving, immovable, the Ātman is eternal." *Gītā*, 2.24.

9. "Look at the waves in the sea. Not one wave is really different from the sea, but what makes the wave apparently different? Name and form; the form of the wave and the name which we give to it, 'wave.' This is what makes it different from the sea. When name and form go, it is the same sea. Who can make any real difference between the wave and the sea? So this whole universe is that one Unit Existence; name and form have created all these various differences." CW, 2. 274–75.

"The whole ocean is present at the back of each wave, and all manifestations are waves, some very big, some small; yet all are the ocean in their essence, the whole ocean; but as waves each is a part. When the waves are stilled, then all is one." CW, 7. 61.

10. "The whole of the universe, therefore, is, as it were, a peculiar form; the Absolute is that ocean while you and I, the suns and the stars, and everything else are various waves of that ocean. And what makes the waves different? Only the form, and that form is time, space, and causation, all entirely dependent on the wave. As soon as the individual gives up this māyā, it vanishes for him and he becomes free." CW, 2. 136.

11. "Science has proved that physical individuality is a delusion, that really my body is one little continuously changing body in an unbroken ocean of matter." CW, 1. 14.

"Today it has been demonstrated that you and I, the sun, the moon, and the stars are but the different names of different spots in the same ocean of matter, and that this matter is continuously changing in its configuration. This particle of energy that was in the sun several months ago may be in the human being now; tomorrow it may be in an animal, the day after tomorrow it may be in a plant. It is ever coming and going. It is all one unbroken, infinite mass of matter, only differentiated by names and forms. One point is called the sun; another, the moon; another, the stars; another, man; another, animal; another, plant; and so on. And all these names are fictitious; they have no reality, because the whole is a continuously changing mass of matter." CW, 2. 276.

12. "This very same universe, from another standpoint, is an ocean of thought, where each one of us is a point called a particular mind. You are a mind, I am a mind, everyone is a mind; and the very same universe viewed from the standpoint of knowledge, when the eyes have been cleared of delusions, when the mind has become pure, appears to be the unbroken Absolute Being, the ever pure, the unchangeable, the immortal." CW, 2. 276.

"There is a continuity of mind, as the yogīs call it. The mind is universal. Your mind, my mind, all these little minds, are fragments of that universal mind, little waves in the ocean; and on account of this continuity, we can convey our thoughts directly to one another." CW, 2. 13.

13. "Upon [the Ātman] name and form have painted all these dreams; it is the form that makes the wave different from the sea. Suppose the wave subsides, will the form remain? No, it will vanish. The existence of the wave was entirely dependent upon the existence of the sea, but the existence of the sea was not at all dependent upon the existence of the wave. The form remains so long as the wave

remains, but as soon as the wave leaves it, it vanishes, it cannot remain. This name and form is the outcome of what is called māyā. It is this māyā that is making individuals, making one appear different from another. Yet it has no existence." CW, 2. 275.

14. Shortly after meeting Sri Ramakrishna, Swami Vivekananda had a mystic vision of the infinite ocean of consciousness and, for a few days after that, everything appeared to him to be made of "one stuff." See His Eastern and Western Disciples, *The Life of Swami Vivekananda*, 2 vols. (Kolkata: Advaita Ashrama, 1979), 1: 96–97.

15. "The Ātman is below. The Ātman is above. The Ātman is behind. The Ātman is in front. The Ātman is to the right. The Ātman is to the left. The Ātman is, indeed, all this." *Chāndogya Upaniṣad*, 7.25.2.

"The immortal brahman alone is in front. Brahman is behind, Brahman is to the right and the left. Brahman alone pervades everything above and below. This universe is the supreme Brahman alone." *Muṇḍaka Upaniṣad*, 2.2.11.

16. "You are only one; there is only one such Self, and that one Self is you. Standing behind this little nature is what we call the Self. There is only one Being, one Existence, the ever-blessed, the omnipresent, the omniscient, the birthless, the deathless. ... Wherever there are two, there is fear, there is danger, there is conflict, there is strife. When it is all one, who is there to hate, who is there to struggle with? When it is all one, with whom can you fight? This explains the true nature of life; this explains the true nature of being. This is perfection, and this is God. As long as you see the many, you are under delusion.... You are the one Being in the universe." CW, 2. 235–36.

17. "Look at the 'ocean' and not at the 'wave.'" CW, 7. 7.

18. Looking at the "ocean" and ignoring the "wave" is a powerful jñāna yoga practice. Chanting of Upaniṣadic texts helps us hold on to the ocean image. For instance the following: "The supreme light [of consciousness] which shines as the substratum of the liquid element—I am that supreme light. I am that supreme light of Brahman which shines as the inmost essence of all the exists. I am the infinite Brahman ["the ocean of consciousness"] even when I am experiencing myself as a limited self ['wave'] due to ignorance. Now I know that I am really Brahman and that is my true nature. I offer my false, limited self into the fire of Brahman, my true, infinite self." *Mahānārāyaṇa Upaniṣad*, 1. 67.

19. For someone on a predominantly devotional path, this may be modified to, for instance, "I am a child of God."

20. "The true jñānis are those who have the deepest love within their hearts and at the same time are practical seers of nonduality in

their outward relations." CW, 5. 318.

21. "What is left attached to the man who has reached the Self and
seen the truth is the remnant of the good impressions of past life,
the good momentum. Even if he lives in a body and works
incessantly, he works only to do good; his lips speak only
benediction to all; his hands do only good works; his mind can only
think good thoughts; his presence is a blessing wherever he goes.
He is himself a living blessing. Such a man will, by his very
presence, change even the most wicked persons into saints. Even if
he does not speak, his very presence will be a blessing to mankind."
CW, 2. 284.

22. See, for instance, *Gītā* 2. 55–72, 12. 13–20 and 14. 22–27, and
Śaṅkarācārya's *Vivekacūḍāmaṇi*, 426–40.

23. See Śaṅkarācārya's commentary on the *Gita*, 2. 54.

24. "This is the only way to reach the goal, to tell ourselves, and to tell
everybody else, that we are divine. And as we go on repeating this,
strength comes. He who falters at first will get stronger and
stronger, and the voice will increase in volume until the truth takes
possession of our hearts, and courses through our veins, and
permeates our bodies. Delusion will vanish as the light becomes
more and more effulgent, load after load of ignorance will vanish,
and then will come a time when all else has disappeared and the
Sun alone shines." CW, 2. 202.

25. "A cloud is here; another comes and pushes it aside and takes its
place. Still another comes and pushes that one away. As before the
eternal blue sky, clouds of various hue and color come, remain for
a short time and disappear, leaving it the same eternal blue, even so
are you, eternally pure, eternally perfect. You are the veritable
Gods of the universe; nay, there are not two—there is but One."
CW, 2. 251.

26. "There is no 'I' nor 'you'; it is all one. It is either all 'I' or all 'you.'
This idea of duality, of two, is entirely false, and the whole
universe, as we ordinarily know it, is the result of this false
knowledge. When discrimination comes and man finds there are
not two but one, he finds that he is himself this universe." CW,
2. 275.

ABOUT THE AUTHOR

A monk of the Ramakrishna Order since 1976, Swami Tyagananda is the head of Ramakrishna Vedanta Society, Boston, and Hindu Chaplain at Harvard and MIT. He has written, edited and translated fourteen books.

ALSO BY SWAMI TYAGANANDA

Walking the Walk: A Karma Yoga Manual

Looking Deeply: Vivekacūḍāmaṇi

A Drop of Nectar: Amritabindu Upanishad

Insights from the Gita (*Audio*)

Kathopanishad (*Audio*)

Narada Bhakti Suta (*Audio*)

Made in the USA
Middletown, DE
29 April 2024